*Faces of the past: Gus Conte, Seamus Fe
Maynard, Frances Howlett, David Heafe
John Anthony, Leo Colston, Micheal O'Bri
Grace, Terence Quinn, John Potter, Angelo
Nicholas Conway, Eddie Satherthwaite, Br
ny Pater, John O'Connor, Michael Docher
Burns, Miss Marie Damon, Jimmy Ashton,
Alan Watson, Michael Lynch, Jeremy Pauli
Paulie, John Waldron, Peter Jones, George
Fitzpatrick, John Delaney, Lawrence Garf
sey, Ronnie Fields, Ian Crangle, Miss Mau
Billy Pieri, Kevin Seaward, Harry Mills, Be
ence Fawkin, Stephen Lamb, Terry Karala
Mullins, Fatty Ryan, Philip Donneky, John
Bleach, Harold Frawly, Mr Mash, Kevin F
Sheppard, Clifford Shaw, Sister Louise, Ju
ne Maronie, John Holmes, Chris Stevens
Hilda, Miss Carmella, Nicky Crangle, Mis
Sister Teresa, Henry Escarcelle, Brian Ho
Margaret, Tony Kavanah, A. Papazoglou,*

my
soul
has
no
friends

a childhood remembered

by Paul C Delrue

First Published in Great Britain by Paul C Delrue 2013.

Edited by Jamie Russell.
Sub editing by Simeon Jones, Heather Harrison, Roz Hulse and Adam Jurkojc.
Typeset in 18/12pt Cambria by Jamie Russell at Delrue Bookbinders, Ruthin 2012.

Photographs by Adam Jurkojc, Patrick Dransfield, Michael O'Brian, Jamie Russell,
Terance Baldock, Dick Quinton, Penny Paulie, Jeremy Paulie, Jimmy Ashton, Salvatore
Celano and countless others, too numerous to name here.

Cover design by Mel Jefferson and Jamie Russell.
End paper montages by Jamie Russell.

Printed and bound by Printing Express Ltd, Hong Kong.

Acknowledgements.

Thanks to friends, without them my book 'My Soul Has No Friends' would still be in an old school exercise book.

Roz Hulse
Heather Harrison
and
Jamie Russell

———————————

The Crusade of Rescue and Homes for Destitute Catholic Children:
Father George, Canon Flood, Father Harvey.
Little Sister Theresa, Sister Philomena, Sister Gabriel, Sister Rosalie, Sister Joseph (Joey), and Sister Kevin, the best cook in the world.
———————————

Miss Driscoll my teacher from St Lawrence's Primary School and the only real saint I have ever met, Miss Hilda Taylor Moore. And the boys; James Ashton, Jeremy Paulie, Frank McGrath and Ian McGregor.

———————————

Friends that have stopped by to tie up their shoe laces:
Reg Denham, Joe Brunton, John Vivian, John Coleman,
Ray & Joan Camp and Geoff Brown.

For
Harry Archmooty Bohum Devereaux, Arnold Strange and Matthew Dome.

And finally my mother,
LOUISE DELRUE, for giving me *Life*.

Paul Charles Delrue.

Born 6th July 1944, Edmonton- County of Middlesex.
Spent two years from birth at Guildford Institution
Taken into care with the Crusade of Rescue in 1946, with medical
form, identity card, ration book and clothing coupons. Placed at
St Vincent's, Feltham.
Sent to St Joseph's, Enfield in 1955.
In July 1959 I went to live with my Mother in Putney, London.
(My many years looked after by the Crusade of Rescue, ended
mostly, a happy childhood.)

Guildford Institution, 1944. Paul (circled) with his mother and and sister Simone. A babe in arms.

Melancholic Boy at St Vincent's.

*I was a serious, thoughtful and somewhat melancholic
boy at St Vincent's Boys' Home; growing up with
hundreds of other boys.*

I was different from the start.

*I played in the playground on my own, my boy thoughts
to myself, my world to myself, carefree and sadly wild.
I was amongst friends,
I was in the company of other boys.*

Foreword by David Rutter.

David Rutter

In spite of all the years as a successful Designer Bookbinder with a large following, Paul Delrue has always been known to me as just one of the many boys brought up in a children's home. Of all the boys I knew, Paul has been the only one with whom I have maintained contact over the last fifty or more years. I have watched his progress from the days when he was an apprentice in the Bindery at Flaxman House, University College London. Throughout that period it is not so much his progress in the world of Designer Bookbinding that has impressed me, impressive though that is, but his knowledge of classical music and other areas of the arts and with it the delightful way he is able to express his love and dislikes to those fortunate to be in his company.

All the more impressive are his accomplishments when I recollect that practically all of us from the children's home were virtually illiterate and inarticulate, unable to express our thoughts and feelings in any coherent way. What was worst we were untutored in the social skills necessary for negotiating our way through the most basic aspects of daily life with its accompanying embarrassments and shame.

Paul's account of his life as a child brought up in a children's home and beyond is both moving and honest. In particular the account of his experiences as a result of ignorance and callous indifference on the part of some of those in whose charge he was placed. As is sometimes the case however, Paul's talents were recognised by kind and perceptive individuals who gave him just the break he desperately needed. Paul and I shared many of the joys and pains that he recalls both at St Vincent's and St Joseph's. It is therefore interesting to find how close our recollections are.

This book however is not just a recollection of those experiences but of how they had shaped his innermost feelings, which make this book such a personal testimony. Throughout the book certain episodes and places are marked out with distinct nostalgia and rightly so. They form major landmarks in a narrative that meanders through the life of a person whose childhood was so one-sided in its distribution of good fortune.

Although life was secure in the basic needs, the one thing lacking was affection. Surprising as it may seem, affection was not something we craved for, rather it simply did not feature in our reckoning on what counted as good fortune. Good fortune for us was to escape physical punishment which was a constant feature when we were very young and, as we got older, to be allowed out into town or to the much loved open spaces of Hilly Fields.

This lack of affection was so ingrained that most of us from the Home found it difficult to respond to any affection when visited upon us after we left the Home.

There is much documentation on the lives of children in a children's home and many have some idea what it must have been like in such care. I doubt, however whether one can penetrate the most intimate aspects of such an experience. Paul's book goes a long way to reveal those aspects and its great strength is that it does not attempt to give an objective account of life in the home, rather it seeks to reveal those impressions which remain with him after such a long time. It is a book not so much on how it was but rather on how he felt it was.

Paul Delrue

Hidden in Words.

Tell me Paul, why are you writing this book, this short run, and who will want to read it? It will certainly not make a better bookbinder of you, by your own admission you're a lousy teacher and have never been able to explain yourself, but maybe you do have something to say.

As a Designer Bookbinder, (as you say again) you are lightweight and will be the first to admit you can only bind to your feelings, but is that good enough? Who will collect your bindings? You bound your first book when you were just 15 – who has that book? I expect you gave it away to another hard up boy from that home you always keep on about. The boys' home I mean. What is so special about you?

Brought up in a boys' home until you were 15 years old, so what? What makes you stand out in any way? Your stories are just your faded memories – who will believe them? You were always good at telling stories, even at school. So, you didn't have a father, wake up Paul, do you want sympathy? You won't get it from me. I just want the truth.

Why are you writing this book? What's eating you? You were mostly happy at St Vincent's and Joey's and quite good at lessons and football. The kids liked you and you were popular and made friends easily... Be honest and say what you mean, be truthful and don't feel sorry for yourself. You always felt the underdog that needed to be heard, perhaps you have something to say, but need time, and that, no one can give you. What is it? You're coming to middle old age – say what you mean.

You might be a better bookbinder than most – you certainly are original. You say you are not collectable and that you don't have a recognisable style, but what does that mean? Your work Paul has heart and feeling; I know it's all about your injustice and you're still angry inside. What are you trying to say after all these years? Perhaps you feel you are a failure and you still suffer some kind of guilt. Why take it upon yourself? What is it you don't say in your book, but only imply, just hint at?

I've come back Paul. Who are you writing this book for and why? I find it a little too much about you and perhaps morbid and grey. What keeps biting away at you? Be truthful for the first time, please, you'll never get another chance, remember you will have your thoughts in writing for ever; there can be no going back.

Why carry this extra burden? Even after all these years, you cannot blame yourself for the many boys from the home who didn't quite make it, who suffered misunderstanding and such painful loneliness, who didn't have the security of the family. Is that what you want to say in your book? Free yourself Paul. Help me, please help me. I can Paul. You have been given such magical hands of expression, let them do the talking, your head is a mind full of beautiful images, let them out slowly; let us all take it in, let us breath your words. What, after these many years, are you still hiding and afraid of saying? Read in these leaves the truth of what makes you tick. I will in turn promise to write it without anger, just the Delrue way.

It happened when I was at St Lawrence's School when I was ten years of age, free and carefree, joyful and happy. It has always made me think how fair the world seemed to me back then. It was all talk; exciting talk in the playground. Who was going to win and become the Heavyweight Champion of the World? I wished and hoped Don Cockell would fight the fight of his life and become the World Champion by beating Rocky Marciano. The tough American boxer had never lost. Don Cockell battled bravely; he put up a gallant fight. It was a slogging match from start to finish, how he tried though. My favourite boxer, Don Cockell, was knocked out in round nine, but what a fight he put up. He ended up being my hero. He

'An angelic mind that was certainly illuminated by heavenly light.'

was floored again and again, but got up again and again, he was an honest man, a trier and he gave his best, but was battered to a pulp by a much better fighter. He was a loser though; his body was battered and bruised in the end. It was a sad finish, but he really tried, he fought a losing battle. I can't help but admire the gifted boxer, Don Cockell.

I dedicate my few leaves to all boys who tried to overcome their personal hardships to live with a generous spirit and bring softness and care to their families and friends. Letters to unfair losers in life. That's all, I promise. I have always found difficulties with winners at all costs. I feel empathy with honest losers. I have looked at life differently.

That's why the book.

'I long to bind beautifully and be remembered for it. Just one book, a deeply private work, an edition of life, a first.' Delrue.

When I was Four.

St.Vincent's Boys' Home, Feltham.

I first understood words at the age of four. They sounded and coloured my imagination, but best of all they could be read. It happened like this: We were all playing in the playground. As always I was happily thinking on my own, playing with my thoughts, thinking how beautiful the Sisters could knit. They used brightly coloured wool to make gloves, scarves, socks, ties and woollen hats; all coloured and gleaming, the yellows and browns were my favourite. I would watch the sisters knitting for hours as they used the needles simply and quickly to make a bagful of wool into something magical. If only I could have a go, but I could not waste their valuable coloured wool.

I watched their skill and it never left me. I soon became the best knitter at St Vincent's. They quickly understood how very keenly I was looking at them, noisily clicking away with their plastic knitting needles. I began making striped ties first, but I found difficulty when knitting gloves and was soon asking Sister for help, which she always sweetly gave. I could never capture her natural abilities with her woollen skills, but I loved watching her as she played around with patterns. Oh, the skill of it all I longed for, but it did come, slowly. Best of all was my simple pleasure of enjoying it, making something useful with my hands.

I understood that words had meanings: I was playing dreamily in the familiar playground along with all the other boys. We were called in as it began to rain. It quickly flooded the playground and all the boys made a rush for cover. I did not hear the boys and Sisters say;

"Paulie, quickly get undercover, you will get wet!"

I was sitting on my own in the middle of the grey, very wet playground with my legs crossed, not taking notice of the many safety calls. I had turned off the overwhelming noise around, I did not hear a thing. At last I understood what words meant to me as the rain water covered me all over, my hair and play clothes were wet through. I licked the water that fell from my eyes and face. I slowly wiped away the rain from my play clothes and legs; and what was I thinking while every body was calling me in to shelter? Rain meant wet. I could feel the wet all over. The rain water felt beautiful as it covered me from head to toe, but not to worry, I could dry off. I was never told off for being wet through; the Sisters were kind and understanding. They undressed me, took my wet clothes to the laundry room, rubbed me down roughly with a soft towel, dried my hair to its original colour and gave me a new set of warm play clothes. I was never caught in the (wet) rain ever again.

'I'd give all wealth that years have piled,
The slow result of life's decay,
To be once more a little child,
For one Bright Summer-day.'

I soon discovered colours. The sun always shone warmly yellow while rain was silvery white and grey, clouds were mostly grey but could be a beautiful rich orange. I could colour flowers in the colour of boys play clothes. The Sisters wore dark blue robes with white stiff coronets and rosary beads hanging from their waist. They were coloured with a cream cross figure of Jesus. I could see colour all around, my eyes bright blue where my best friend Jeremy's eyes were sadly brown. He had black hair while I had fair hair and pale skin. The boys' home was awash with colour. I loved colouring books, my favourite being my crayoning book with my own made up stories. Bath time was never the same again; the water started off whitish and ended up dirty light brown. Two by two the boys went into the bath, soaped down with a

Paulie at four.

6

flannel, then moved onto the Sister who washed the suds from their soapy bodies with much splashing of water. Out of the bath we would come, to be dried off and ready for Sunday Mass, looking pure and clean. Hair brushed and in our best clothes, we were fit for Mary and Jesus at St Anthony's Church.

We would kneel down, close our eyes and put our hands together and pray sincerely for the kindness around us. I had just received my first Holy Communion, so I felt truly and deeply about God Almighty, the true saviour of the world. I would kneel on the polished benches, close my eyes and put my hands over my face, praying and thinking holy thoughts, honouring my prayers and longing for Holy Communion, which would be part of me; the body and blood of Jesus, our Lord, our Loving Saviour. I lived in his thoughts throughout my years in the boys' home.

St Vincent's driveway looking out onto Faggs Road, Feltham.

After Mass we would quickly walk through the woods, returning to St Vincent's Home, have a quick wash and then a breakfast of porridge or cornflakes, a slice of white bread and margarine with a mug of warm milk. The food never changed, not even at Christmas or Easter. After breakfast we would say grace of thanks. We would then go to the school rooms (thirty five boys at a time). There were four school rooms. They had plainly painted walls of light brown and cream with pictures of

Bible scenes all around the room. We would start school at nine am with morning prayers and Bible reading (which I truly enjoyed). The stories were exciting and colourful, perhaps bloody. I loved hearing the stories of the Saints, who all died a marked death, a terrible death. How could they take such pain, always to die; stones, lions' den, plagues, starvation, hanging, eyes pulled out, spears to the heart, boiling water. But I enjoyed learning about it; it thrilled me that so many could die for a cause, for God Almighty. Jesus, his mother Mary and father Joseph kept me together. They were without sin, I worshipped them. The Christmas story was my favourite, I fell in love with the poor shepherd but not the three wise men; the Kings who lived on gold that I could never understand. Why would baby Jesus want gold and riches? Surely he would want more straw and warm blankets.

'More sunlight in a Single Song.'

After Bible reading it was time for lessons. I enjoyed reading aloud. The boys enjoyed listening to me; I had a light shiny voice. The bell would ring for dinner, it never changed. The dinners were mostly boiled meat and potatoes, together with cabbage or butter beans, frogspawn or rice pudding a mug of warm milk, a grace of thanks, a quick wash of the face and hands and return to the classroom. We mostly started the afternoon painting or drawing. I drew with coloured pencils; mountains and hills, a neat red brick built house with a tall chimney smoking. There were curtains in the windows, a bright green front door and in front a small boy with a hat on (about my age). He would be waiting to be let in, but the green door was always closed. The small boy never knew what the inside of the house looked like. He was always sad. I wish I could have painted him smiling. It was always the garden fences that spelled danger. The boy was afraid of wooden fences. He sometimes had a tear in his eye. I would draw birds in the sky free and together, singing, flying from the cold countries to warmer countries like The Gold Coast or Egypt. My birds were happy and carefree, how would I ever paint happy? But as I drew I felt it, they were sometimes very colourful when their wings were completely open, their beaks were brightly yellow. They never pecked at the smaller birds. They flew country to country, always friends, the smaller birds were sometimes lifted up, sleeping on white, warm, bubbly clouds. They were in bird heaven, let them rest.

We then had tea and a slice of bread and Echo. Lessons ended with reading and writing. I enjoyed poetry reading or copying poems into my lined school writing book. We finished with history; stories of kings and queens and the British winning all rightful wars for the sake of that much over used word, freedom. Listening to the teachers all day wore us out. The bell rang. We put away our history books in our desks and cleaned out our ink nibs and pots. Leaving quickly two by two, out of the classroom, going upstairs to the dormitories, changing our school clothes for play clothes, (all done quickly and quietly) and walking downstairs to the playground where the fun began. Rounders with the girl helpers, cowboys riding on horses, running around and playing tick. I always played with the same three boys, who were to become my best friends. We were good at shoulder backs; fighting much bigger boys than ourselves. We were inseparable, fighting and sticking up for each other. We were the goodies fighting off the bullies, always keeping an eye out for the smaller boys, helping the new kids who came to St Vincent's for the first time and were homesick. But what was meant by homesickness? We never had a mum or dad or a home.

St Vincent's Boys' Home was full of song. I first heard singing in the boot room with the Irish helpers; they hummed the latest popular hit songs we had heard on the wireless. As the helpers worked cleaning and tidying the large home they would always be singing. It soon caught on to us boys who would join in encouraged by the Sisters. They never sang songs like us boys. It would be the tunes I could easily hum, the words came later. But we would sing at our best in the boot room. The shoes were stored there, black and brown, boots with sandals and plimsoles to the ready. Boys always had growing feet and holey socks, changed just once a week like our vests, linings and pyjamas, but did it matter? We were mostly clean boys.

The first ever songs I remember were: 'The Old Folks at Home', 'Did You Ever See a Dream Walking', 'Play a Simple Melody' and 'Swanny River'. I remember singing clearly and loudly with such enthusiasm. My favourite singing time was when all the boys waited in the large playroom for our monthly haircut, we would sing our hearts out: 'The Shoemakers Song', 'Now is the Hour', 'Frostie the Snowman', 'My Heart Cries for You', the pot boilers of the day. The girl helpers truly came into their own. They sang all the latest hits, we would just follow in the simple pleasure.

Hilly Fields, Enfield.

It could not last. When we left St Vincent's; at 11 years old, moving to St Joseph's Boys' Home in Enfield. Our singing together days were over. I think I missed community singing at St Vincent's more than anything. Enfield was much larger and the boys older, therefore more frightening. It was all sport, learning to grow up, my boy days were over, I believed in Jesus less and it could never be the same. I felt fear for the first time. I finish living in the boys' home in Enfield turning just 15 years. I remember the home with its friendships, bunking into the picture houses, walking slowly along the New River and playing all summer long at Hilly Fields. I remember walking two miles to Enfield swimming baths, playing football with Tony Kavanagh under the laundry roof, walking to St George's School and meeting outside boys and girls (who lived in a normal family home) for the first time. Stealing from Enfield Town High Street shops, broken biscuits, palm toffee, it all comes back.

Altar boys ready for latin lessons.

11

Best of all were my three friends at St Vincent's in the late '40s and early '50s. I look back on my childhood as almost perfect, a warm feeling, going to church and singing in the choir at Christmas time, serving at the altar, giving the Sisters Holy Communion, ringing the three bells, answering Father Stibbs in latin and passing the Holy wine and water. I was eager and wide eyed, sensitive and mostly loved.

Memories from the boys' home 1949-1959.

Tea with Miss Driscoll *of St. Lawrence's School.*

Just before I had reached 11 years old, I, along with my three best friends were invited to the school teachers' home for tea at 4 o'clock prompt. Miss Driscoll met our soft knock at her front door smiling, and welcomed us into her home in Feltham High Street, next to the duck pond. Her house was painted yellow and cream, it felt homely, warm, and strange. We walked on carpets for the first time. She lead us into her tea room (I learnt later that it was called a dining room). I'd never been into a house

Miss. Driscoll, my favourite teacher.

where people lived. We had never seen so many books, but it was the wallpaper that caught my eye, all flowers, lightly coloured. Each room was different, even the lavatory which was small and brightly coloured. We had never seen anything like it. I pulled the chain for the first time. It made a quiet noise and I used toilet paper which was hanging on a wall holder, for the first time. There was even a lock on the inside of the door.

Miss Driscoll and her sister had prepared tea for us boys. We looked smart in our school uniform, with clean grey shirts, school socks and a blazer. We all look a picture of pride to be invited to our school teacher's house, which she shared with her older sister who was also a school teacher in Hatton Cross; I remember that she drove a blue motor car. She was kind to us boys, smiled and understood our difficulty in seeing her home for the first time.

Just before tea she asked us if we might like to see her garden, which was full of small coloured flowers, roses and a

Sister Bernard and the Pupils of St Lawrence's School 1953.

finely cut green lawn with a table and chairs resting on it. She brought out a tray if lemonade and biscuits. We were polite and took just one biscuit, although we were offered more. It was time for tea; we were all a little nervous at the idea of a posh tea. We had never drunk from finely cut teacups and saucers with their matching plates. The tea set was white with daisies along the edge and felt so smooth to the touch, we were most careful to hold our cups securely. Would we like a sugar lump in our tea, perhaps two? We were passed sugar tongs. Then came the sandwiches of beef and fish paste, again it was all new to us. The sandwiches were cut and quartered, very tasty indeed and we finished off with a large Victoria sponge cake with cream and strawberry jam filling. It was delicious and we all had a second helping. Tea ended with marshmallow rolls covered in chocolate; we had never eaten so well. It was nearly six o'clock and time to catch the 90B bus and return home to St Vincent's.

I now look back and remember that posh tea with Miss Driscoll and her sister in their house on Feltham High Street. I was with my greatest friends. We shared that early evening tea and those new experiences; all that was good and kind, and I loved that day, but I never got to use sugar tongs ever again. We smiled and laughed a lot, what more can you ask? We saw inside a house for the first time! I will always remember the flowery wallpaper and super tea.

open it fully, it was too heavy.

"Paulie, give it a shove, go on!"

I shoved it with all my might, the door opened fully. In the far end of the large room, a figure, black suited, with a big warm smile.

"Paulie, who do we have here?"

I looked a second time.

"Why Paulie, it's your Mother."

I looked for a third time, shyly smiling, and ran towards her. I was in her arms, secure and happy.

I was in heaven.

17

Our Fathers.

All I ever knew was that I had grown up and that I had a mother, nothing more. It was years before I ever gave a thought that I had a father. I had lived with the knowledge that he had been a parachutist and had been killed over France in late 1944. He had been killed fighting for King and Country, like so many young men. He would have been nearly nineteen years old. May he rest in peace like so many of our young, dying for a cause he could not perhaps understand. My mother had met him in The Coach and Horses in Chiswick. He fell in love with an older woman of twenty three. They were together for just seven months, before he was sent abroad. That is all I grew up with, a war hero, a silent partner, my mothers war lover, like so very many. They wrote many letters, love letters, simple letters longing for the day he would come home to Chiswick to marry his sweetheart. That of course never happened.

My mother was a Roman Catholic (although not a practicing one) and not able to look after me. As a babe in arms I was sheltered from the world for 15 years. I felt secure and happy, I was to know no other life than mixing with two hundred other boys, all looked after by kindly Sisters of Charity, dedicating

The boys of St Vincent's 1952, my first Feltham home.

The boys and the ducks with little Sister Theresa.

themselves to a Christian cause. The Church played a big part in my life. I was to serve as an Altar boy, wearing cassocks, ringing bells and answering Father Stibbs in Latin verse. It came easy to me; I loved serving at the altar and giving Father the water and wine. I never felt as near to God as when I served him at St Vincent's Church, singing his praises aloud and with true feeling. A beautiful experience, reciting prayers with other boys and Sisters, meaning all words sincerely truthfully and with simple honesty. My eyes were opened to all that was good about the home. I lived for Sundays. I went to confession every two weeks. At times I found it difficult, what could I confess? Stealing, spitting, staring at other boys or Sisters and perhaps a dirty mind or blowing off in Church, but nothing of this was the truth. I made it up, I had to say something. I was a true Christian and never asked Jesus for anything, not even good weather when we went on seaside trips to Littlehampton, Dymchurch and Brighton. It was not right to be selfish and ask Jesus for gifts of chocolate and boiled sweets or cream soda. I lied in the confessional box but said my penance

'There is a god Who nods off to the lullaby of hosannas.' of prayers anyway. Why oh Lord do I have to say things that hurt you and me? I don't understand. I looked at the many statues of the Saints for answers; particularly St Teresa holding Rosary beads in her lovely hands. She always answered me by smiling saying just try to be good and truthful. I loved her. But I grew up and my innocence left me. Joy and happiness were never to be given again.

The world had lied, and the biggest lie of all: My hero father was alive and living with his family in Coventry, but that journey took me five years of looking. Jack Spencer Payne was born in Brighton early 1924 and married in 1948. I was without a father all of these years. I feel cheated, for I would have loved a father. He would hold my hands tightly, take me to the park to play, take me to football matches, he would guide me and talk softly, giving me good advice. I would be tucked up in a secure bed, in a family house and he would kiss me goodnight;

20

"Remember to say your prayers and be thankful."

I miss the love he would have given to me. When I was ill he would stay awake and be there when I woke up. He would

St Joseph's Playground (under the laundry roof).

The boys of St Joseph's gathering in the evening sun.

worry about me, smile and laugh a lot, encourage me to be a good boy. But, most of all I would have loved to say;

"Dad." or "It's Dad."

"Dad's home, let's go for a walk before tea, remember your grandparents will be joining us."

My grandfather would be honest and wise and my grandmother would be full of sensible advice and say;

"My son, you can only do your best. At school, teacher tells me you're good with your hands and really quite a painter, and that your English is very good."

But it's nothing more than a daydream, a fantasy. It was cruel to be without a father, it hurt, life is not what it might have been. Perhaps I might have followed him into the motor car industry and not taken up bookbinding, after all most fathers and sons follow the family. My Grandfather also worked in the car industry, firstly at Brighton, then Coventry to spend the rest of his life working nights in the factory. How I would have hated that.

Hidden Tears.

Golden Boy, a self portrait of a first born SON, which loving and supportive parents placed upon their young boy.

Drilling into him from an early age, that failure is not an option and his tears are a sign of weakness. Feeling evermore unable to meet their high demands, he soldiers on, continuously trying hard not to disappoint, doing his best to get gold stars and to be their good SON.

Inside he hides his fear of failing and self loathing, knowing that expressing emotion is not acceptable, thinking himself to be a 'let down' and weak for feeling this way to start with.

Trying increasingly harder not to disappoint he keeps up his role, hiding behind his smiling, shining gilded mask, his quiet despair,

Loneliness and his hidden tears.

Paul with Benny the cat.

Tea with Mother.
St. Vincent's Home 1951.

"He never speaks very much, only smiles when I go and fetch him and only talks to say what he would like to eat." (A direct quote from my mother, found on my personal Crusade of Rescue file).

My mother asked the Sister Superior of St Vincent's Home if she could spend the day with Paul, her son, and take him out to tea on Saturday 19th May 1951. Sister told my mother that it would be in order as she has not seen him for many months. Paul was always asking;

"When am I going to see my mother?"

My mother was sent a Visitors Permit by Father George. I was met by her at St Vincent's, and with her holding my right hand tightly we walked across the road to the bus stop. We waited for the 90B bus which would take us to Feltham High Street, for tea in a place known as 'Joe's Café'. I was excited. We sat down together and the bus conductor gave my mother two bus tickets; a brown ticket for her and a grey one for me. He handed the grey children's ticket to me but my mother took it from me. I asked her if I could have it back as I collect bus tickets, along with my three best friends, and we play flick card games every day in the playground. She did

Louise Delrue.

not reply and put my ticket in her handbag. She carried sweets and cigarettes; it was always bulky and full. She just smiled and offered me a peardrop to suck on. I did not know what to say to her and was a little afraid.

"Thank you." I said.

She looked at me and smiled a big wide smile on her lovely face; I was always comforted by her lovely smile, but did not know what to say.

"Please don't do that you are getting on my nerves."

I stopped humming at once; when ever I was worried I turned to humming as comfort. *Must remember not to hum in front of my mother in case it upsets her!* I was happy when the bus conductor rang the bell and told us ours was the next stop. I looked at my mother worriedly.

"Paul, off we go. I expect tea will be ready for us and remember Paul, you choose whatever you would like."

We entered Joes Café and sat down at the table near the front window. It had a check table cloth, clean and bright, just like the dining room at the boys home.

"Paul what would you like to eat?"

I asked for spam and chips with tomato sauce, and to drink I had powdered lemonade. I forget what my mother had but I remember that while we waited for our food, she opened up her bulky handbag full of sweets and bus tickets, and took out a packet of cigarettes known as 'Players Weights'. She then retrieved a box of matches and lit up, smoking into my small, pale face. It made me feel a little sickly. I turned my face away, pretending to look out of the window at the people passing by.

I did not have to wait long before my food came on a small, pale yellow plate, along with a small glass of lemonade. I ate the food slowly not looking at my mother. She lit up once again and sipped her cup of very sweet, milky tea which she had together with a slice of fruit cake. I was feeling cold in the café and was pleased I'd kept my school coat on. Mother handed me a napkin to wipe my face with. I think the sisters would have been very pleased with me, for I was well mannered and always remembered my 'please' and 'no thank you'. I thanked the lady who served us and smiled at her on our way out. I looked down and saw the ash tray full of cigarette ends with her lip stick on. It made me quite sick.

"Paul, now what do you say, was that not the best tea you have ever had?" she asked.

"Yes mother, thank you." I answered.

"Don't forget to tell Father George how much you enjoyed your tea with your mother remember!"

25

Feltham High Street, Joe's Cafe.

I looked at mother while crossing the road to the bus stop. I did not know what to say. I found it difficult to talk to her, this stranger called my mother, who I had not seen more than six times in my short life at St Vincent's. I was only seven years old and had just received my first communion last Sunday. I was so happy to be with the other boys who also received their Holy

Communion. My mother never spoke to me, just smiled, telling me about my sister Simone, who was nearly ten years of age.

"Next time I visit you I will bring your sister Simone with me, it will be so very nice to have you both together, won't that be lovely Paul, just to have the three of us together? I must ask Sister when we get back to arrange for a visitors permit for next August Bank Holiday. Perhaps we can go back to my home in Chiswick and visit Aunt Yvonne for tea. Now that would be something to look forward to Paul."

"What is an Aunt?" I asked my mother.

"Don't be silly Paul; your Auntie is my sister and you have never met her."

"Mother, I don't understand, honestly."

She just looked at me and scowled. It was the last time I spoke to her, I was afraid she would slap me across the face, she seemed very angry. Why, I asked myself, I did not understand, it made me very sad, but I did not want to cry in front of this lady who says she is my mother.

I was relieved to see my bus the 90B, which would take me back to St Vincent's Home and my friends and the Sisters. I was happy there. On the way home my mother told me to be a brave boy, to be good to the Sisters and the young girl helpers, and to remember them in my goodnight prayers. She never asked me how I was getting on at Mass now that I was an Altar Boy. She just spoke to me about matters that meant nothing to me. She told me that she had a much younger brother called Paul;

"Just like you, so you can see we have two Paul's in the family."

What family? I had never met Uncle Paul, who is just thirteen, or Aunt Yvonne. Are most families like mine, do they live together, or are they like me? Do some of their kids live in boys or girls homes? There is so much I don't know or understand – *please help me* – but I kept these thoughts to myself. Are all mothers like the one I had? I felt unloved, but what is love? I only know I love the boys, Sisters and helpers at St Vincent's.

Uncle Paul.

The 90B arrived on the dot of 5 O'clock at the boys' home. Sister Superior met us at the large front door, asking me if I enjoyed myself, having tea with my mother. I smiled and said I had enjoyed myself very much. I thanked my mother and hugged and kissed her goodbye. Sister looked at me and realised that I had not liked tea with this lady known as my mother.

27

"Don't worry Paulie, it's nice having you home safely with us, we all missed you. Go along to the playground, you will see your three friends waiting for you."

I ran across to them, jumping into their arms. I held them tight, closing my eyes asking myself is this love, if this is love I never want to let it go.

Tea with my mother by her son, aged 7 years old in 1951.
I never visited my mother's family at Chiswick and I did not see her again until I was nine, two years later. When I saw her again I did not recognise her, this lady in black, known as my mother.

I Never Passed my Ninth Year.
Miss Dora – Irish Helper – St Vincent's Boys' Home - 1952.

This is the most difficult story and the Final I shall write. I first wrote it at my home in Llandudno during May 2006. I have not changed any of the words. It's my story. I have to write it simply, how it happened. I must not make of it more than it was, it must be the truth as I remember it. I am once again that small boy of eight years old, a daydreamer, friendly and even this is his terrible fear that happened, that night, so long ago.
Keep it as it happened:

I have to be right in mind, I can hardly keep it to myself, I have to write it down, I wish it would go away. I've kept the images of my childhood nightmare to myself for long enough. How it still pains me after these many years. I still remember it as clearly as the day it happened. I was an eight year old boy, living in St Vincent's Boys' home in Feltham with many other small boys, looked after by Sisters of Charity and young Irish women helpers. The Sisters were kind to us helpless beings and I lived happily there for many years. I was very frightened of Miss Dora; she bullied me, often hitting me with a wooden coat hanger. I was always naked. Miss Dora took a liking to me. I was her boy and she enjoyed putting fear into me, keeping an eye on me always. I was never free from her.

It was bedtime. All the boys were ready for bed, washed and clean, ready for a nights sleep. The lights went out at eight thirty pm, quiet and peaceful, we were all asleep in seconds. It was a large and bright dormitory, sleeping about thirty boys, row by row, in our metal framed beds, with a comfortable mattress, starched white cotton sheets and warm coloured blankets.

I must tell you what happened next: With the lights off, I saw a dark and shadowy figure showing a little light. The figure was Miss Dora, she slowly came toward my bed, waking me. I was sleepy and suddenly very frightened.

"Quiet, not a word!" she whispered.

I now saw clearly into the dark, this terrible moment. I could not even cry or make a noise, I knew she could make it worse. The lights were out, all I could hear were other boys breathing safely in their beds. I lay in bed in fear and bewilderment, closing my eyes and not moving. What happened next I could hardly believe. Miss Dora moved my stiff small body, removing my pyjama bottoms she turned me on to my right side. She tied woollen string to my willy and then onto the metal frame of the bed. She told me not to move an inch and not say a word to anyone. I have kept my word ever since. I have kept it secret. I slept soundly and dared not move. In the early morning Sister Teresa and the other Sisters roused the dorm. I woke up in total fear, I cried aloud, waking up the whole dormitory. My small body was covered in blood, my tears were red. The Sisters coming to my bed bring with them a bedroom screen. The nurse, Sister Michael, untied the string, which was still holding fast. She wiped me clean. I was taken down to the infirmary, still in shock.

'There are shadows all around me, dark but mostly light.'

29

After many weeks, I washed away the memory of that night. I have wondered over the years if it had happened to another boy, for I cannot face the truth that I was that other boy, so many years ago. I was that small pale boy, the memory is still as clear as it happened.

Has it affected me? Was I ever damaged? I cannot say, but at least I will not take this fear into my death, this dreadful night on my own. I am released from this terrible burden. I was happy as a small boy, but I never passed my ninth year.

Miss Dora was a young Irish helper. I grew up with her always being there. We went on long walks together, played rounders in the playground with the other boys. She was helpful and fun, all the boys liked her, but it was me she liked best of all. She often bathed me, touching me all over, it was more than touching, I could tell by the way she looked at me; naked and shy. I began to hide from her, but she always found me. She asked me to follow her to the linen room, alone. She undressed me, touched me and told me that of all the boys she loved me, saying I was her special boy. I had lived with her since I was five. She never changed, for her it grew into an obsession. I could not understand. Why me? I was just like all the other kids, but I always thought Jesus and Mother Mary would find out and protect me. I kept my linen room nakedness private and I was very afraid of her. She even remembered my birthday, giving me a large bag of broken biscuits with a flowery card;

"With love from Miss Dora, to my special boy Paulie."

All the sisters approved. She was allowed to give me a birthday kiss. And that's it. After this night the Sisters had guessed who had committed this awful act. I never saw her again, perhaps she returned to Ireland. What does it matter? In fact it does

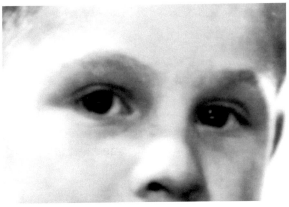

'Never touch INNOCENCE'

matter. That night alone with Miss Dora has haunted me. Still it colours my mind and still I wonder why it happened to me. I'm not a stronger person for that experience, just sad. It has shaken the life out of me, perhaps, it made me what I was to become.

Next time you see someone unusual and quiet,
Remember the snowdrops, the boy, the quiet,
He knew, he realised, I was human and sad,
A person, a someone,
I was so glad.

As I Remember. *The Story of Miss Dora.*

I have finished writing my book of childhood, but I keep returning to my last story, the true story of Miss Dora; 'I Never Passed my Ninth Year'. Somehow it happened as I tell, but I have left out the real truth of my feelings and perhaps love that I clearly held for Miss Dora. I had known her since I was five, she held me spellbound, I was her boy, her special boy; she loved me above all the other boys at St Vincent's Boys' Home. We held onto our love until that terrible night in the month of May 1952. Why did Miss Dora choose me? I was pale, fair and looked like an angel; the Sisters and the boys liked me. I was popular, everyone wanted to be my friend, to hold my hand, to play with me, sit next to me in church. After Mass we always went on our Sunday Walks to Minimax, to play in the park on the swings, roundabouts and slides. The park smelled of fruit for it was near to an orchard. I hated the smell of the orchard; it made me quite sick. I tended to sit quietly, just watching the other boys run around and play. That's it; I loved watching the other boys having fun, laughing a lot, rolling around in the short grass and just being boys, smiling, simply, noisily and looking out for each other.

32

All the boys loved Miss Dora, it was she who joined in the fun; pushing the roundabouts, stretching out for apples and pears, cherries and plums, playing rounder's and shoulderbacks and hiding amongst the fruit trees in the sickly orchard. Miss Dora always looked and smiled at me sitting alone on the park bench. The hour of fun at the Minimax Park came to an end when we walked two by two back to St Vincent's for Sunday Dinner. We all hated Sunday dinner with its cold fatty meat, known as scallywag, grey soft boiled potatoes with butter beans or bright green cold cabbage. We finished off with jelly and junket. After grace of thanks we all, with Miss Dora, went upstairs to change into our play clothes, shorts and T-shirt, with a warm pullover knitted by the Sisters. We played and walked around in many colours of wool.

I kept my special friendship with Miss Dora a secret, even

The boys' dormitory.

from my three best friends. We all shared a summer birthday and would look forward to being nine. It was early evening, after our usual tea of 'dolk' and Echo with strawberry jam and warm milk, we went to the large, noisy, cold bathroom for a strip wash before bedtime. It was the time I looked forward to, the time I spent alone with Miss Dora. It was quiet and free, to be on our own and to be ourselves. The mood rarely changed, I would slip into the small button room and slowly take off my play clothes. I got used to Miss Dora looking at my naked body, touching me all over, warmly and slowly, then gently at first, smacking me with the white wooden coat hanger. I would look fully into her face as she hit me. It hurt, but I took it to be a secret that we shared. She would brush my neat, fair hair from my clear blue eyes. I saw the pleasure on Miss Dora's full round warm face, how I pleased her as she touched me over and over again. Her touch never aroused me. It was clear to me that I meant everything to her; I was Miss Dora's special boy. I would do anything for her kiss on my wanting lips. Miss Dora held me over the soft brown chair, picking up the white wooden coat hanger, she smiled and started to hit me on my bottom, hitting softly at first but with harder strokes following. I just wanted to be Miss Dora's boy. How I needed her love and friendship.

34

I would, even at the age of eight, take any form of punishment to be totally 'her boy', her boy Paulie, her favourite sunny boy, who would do anything she asked of me, she looked at me, holding me tightly as she continued to smack me with the wooden coat hanger. She then laid the hanger down on the soft brown chair. I returned it to its usual place, laying it carefully on the top of the brightly coloured button box lid. After hitting and rubbing my bottom Miss Dora would very gently lift me into a warm bath and wash me with a pink flannel, soaping me all over my body; how I looked forward to her baths. I wished it would never end. She would dry me very gently with her soft white towel.

I never told a soul and kept our love a secret. I would walk around St Vincent's Boys' Home as its king, keeping my inner feelings to myself, wanting more of her affection. These coat hanger smacks took place about once a month. I never got used to them; all I wanted was Miss Dora's love all day and night time long, a simple but loving longing. What did this small eight year old boy see in Miss Dora? She touched me, always giving simple companionship. I was with her all the time; her many long summer walks, just being alone with her, a small boy with a real grown up, sharing secrets. I was comfortable with her at all times, she was there for all the other boy's but I was the special chosen one, out of a hundred boys.

Two years later I was made an Altar Boy and went to confession every two weeks. Telling Father Stibbs of sins that I did not commit, it was easy, I could make it up, lie with an angels smile. I did not understand the punishment for sinning, but I enjoyed quietly praying on every occasion. I was deeply spiritual and spoke to Jesus even when I was playing with my best three friends.

On Saturday afternoon Miss Dora treated me to the Pictures in Feltham High Street, to see my first film; 'To Hell and Back' starring Audie Murphy – a rare treat for any boy at St Vincent's Boys' Home and it was the first time I ever had an ice cream tub. I was indeed the happiest boy alive.

Miss Dora had a fresh round face, a beauty from Dublin. Her light fair hair was naturally curly and her eyes coloured hazel, together with her smile so clear, it smiled to the world of St Vincent's Boys' Home. Miss Dora dressed me to receive my first Holy Communion when I had just turned seven years old. She had bought me a pale white suit for the occasion. I remember the warmth of the tight clinging shorts rubbing against my smooth legs. She had also bought me white woollen socks to match my cream sandals. I felt especially thankful for Miss Dora, and how the Sisters were proud of me! I was the perfect Communicant. I don't think I was ever closer to The Almighty God on High than when I took my first Holy Communion. I slowly made my way to

Paulie's first Holy Communion.

the polished wooden altar pews, taking my place alongside the other boys. I closed my eyes and opening my mouth widely Father gave me the Eucharist. For the first time I was receiving the body and blood of his son Jesus Christ. I wept with joy returning to my pew, with all eyes looking at me. I returned slowly so that everyone could see me in my new communion clothes. I looked up for the approval of one person, Miss Dora. I noticed no other. I made her very proud, for I was ever her boy. That day sealed our special love, a feeling I could not understand.

Miss Dora was taller than the other helpers and I thought her the loveliest. She told me once to keep a secret; it was her birthday, she was twenty. What a secret to keep! Miss Dora always remembered my birthday. I wondered if the other kids were jealous. Yes, my account of my own nightmare at her hand was true as I remember, but I was afraid to let in the real truth, which was my own deeply felt affection that I held for Miss Dora. It was a kind of love on both sides.

Perhaps I was the one who was hurt in the end, but never in my mind did Miss Dora mean to make me bleed and leave me alone. I always trusted her, she never meant to really hurt me. I did as she asked as she secured the woollen string around the side of my metal bed. When Sister Michael carefully unwound the woollen blanket string, so as not to hurt me anymore, it was the first time I experienced true pain and Miss Dora was not there to help. I wanted to tell her it was not her fault, at last I could not help myself and cried and cried thinking I had let Miss Dora down, for I am still your boy, your special boy, believe me please.

I spent many weeks in St Vincent's Boys' infirmary recovering, but my mind was only on Miss Dora, feeling I had let her down. I asked the Sisters please could I see Miss Dora and talk to her.

"Paulie, don't worry we have put everything right, you will never see her again, she can't frighten you ever again. She has returned to her home in Dublin, you are better off trying to get better, the doctor will call and see you again this afternoon. We shall look after you I promise"

I was so unhappy, but after weeks of getting my strength back the Sisters said I could leave the infirmary. On the last day I had a short visit from Miss Maureen, another Irish helper. Miss Maureen handed me a note, telling me to put it away in my back pocket and not to tell the Sisters.

It was on a bright, sunny early June day that I walked slowly out into the familiar playground, across into Farmer Buck's field. I walked to the end of the playing field, looking around for the shaded Green Field that would be private, giving me the whole world to myself. I lay quiet and secretive on the warm grass and putting my hand in my back pocket, I took out the note Miss

Maureen had given me. It said this:

"My Dear Paulie, please forgive me, please forgive me I would never hurt you and make you bleed, I was still proving my love for you and you for me, that's all, can you ever forgive me? I will make it up to you one day, I promise – Paulie my own special lovely boy how I love you. I will surely miss you. I will remember you always."

I looked up into the bright clear blue sky and cried quiet tears. I never seemed to stop, I let out no sound, just tears, thinking how could life ever be the same again, without Miss Dora? My tears began to say I shall never let you go. Miss Dora's note ended with a simple written kiss. The pain, weeks and months later would never leave me. I returned Miss Dora's note to Miss Maureen; she just smiled and thanked me. It was my three friends who got me through her loss, for I was able to weep on their shoulders for a loss they could never understand.

39

I was nine years old in July, somehow I hoped Miss Dora would, as ever, remember me, but I was never to see or hear from her again. At least the years helped and as time goes by, the memory of her loss pains me less and less. It is the first time in sixty years I have shared my four years with the Irish helper Miss Dora to the outside world, not minding if you understood or not. How lucky I was, her eight year old special boy with a simple brave and faithful smile.

Love always, Paulie 1952.

Cotton Wool Clouds - A Dream.

I folded my striped Pyjamas neatly under my pillow together with an elastic band, hidden away from the Sisters and the girl helpers. It was Sunday, late evening, when at seven o'clock (winter) bedtime I dressed into my pyjamas and slid into the warmth and security of my bed, the covers all over me, hiding me away. I waited for the lights in the dormitory to be turned off, leaving me in the dark. I slipped slowly up until my head reached the dim light; all was quiet and I returned to the darkness of my bed covers.

I opened my eyes and from the top pocket of my pyjamas I took my elastic band, my musical secret. I placed one end of the band in my mouth, held it carefully with my front teeth and began pinging up and down. My elastic band made the most beautiful noise, pure holy music, a lovely sound as I stretched my music up and down. With my small fingers I could make a variety of plucking sounds. The darkness of my bed lit up and music bounced off my woollen blanket. It was truly magical, my small fingers plucking my elastic band until I grew tired and worried in case the sisters heard my secret. Only my ears were left to the golden sounds. I slowly and silently pinged my last, making the elastic band drop out onto my right hand and putting it away into my pyjama top pocket. I slipped away to dreamland, to sounds of little Paulie's musical treats. I stayed under my blanket covers and was soon deeply asleep.

I am in heaven, bright, holy and gloriously happy. Could it last? I lay in fear, my small body begins to spin around and around. Slowly at first, around and around I would go, faster and faster. Then rest. I am out of breath but I open my eyes and begin to spin around again; spinning around and around, faster and faster, still the cotton wool clouds follow me, quickly catching me up. The clouds slowly tighten around my whole body, faster and faster. I cannot keep up with the white clouds, they are tightening around my neck, around, around, around I turn. The clouds are strangling me! I am full of pain and sweat,

'Sell back the knowledge, so dearly bought, for the pennies of wonder In a child's thought.'

blood pours out of my eyes but still I spin... I lay clean upon the white clouds, floating, wide awake, pure and simple, holding my elastic band between my front teeth and small hands, making music to the yellow moon and silvery stars. I slowly float between the warm blue clouds, I am in a heavenly, bright and richly coloured land.

I hear claps outside my bed, clapping loudly, I slip out of my warm bed kneeling at its side, saying prayers together with the other boys. Morning prayers, which I hardly understood. I wash and dress, the day is beginning. Monday early to Mass, then breakfast, another quick wash then off to the schoolroom, more prayers, Bible reading, story telling, then dinnertime with Grace of thanks for cold meat, cabbage and grey potatoes, with jelly for afters. Then more prayers, afternoon learning in the painted schoolroom, teatime, playtime then wash before bedtime, night prayers and the fear of my dream.

41

I still have that dream, it never leaves me. Still the white cotton wool clouds, tight around me, strangling me, but still I wake up in the morning. As a child if I woke up with a wet bed I would be hit by the Irish helpers. I've learned to live with my dream.

My Holidays at the Seaside as a Small Boy.
Littlehampton and Dymchurch in the '50s.

Fathers, Sisters and holiday boys.

We all looked forward to our summer holidays by the seaside. For weeks there was nothing but excitement amongst the boys and Sisters. I remember clearly how we shouted aloud when we saw arriving in the front of St Vincent's our coach of cream and green. I had never seen such a coach, so colourful, and we all clambered in along with the Sisters. Sister Veronica asked all the boys for calm, to close our eyes, put our hands together and pray to Saint Christopher (the patron Saint of travel) for a safe journey. With that, we were off for our first ever seaside adventure, singing 'Oh I do Like to be Beside the Seaside'.

We were to stay at Seaford House; an attractive large house which was the Sisters retreat at Littlehampton, where they had kindly set aside enough room for us all. We walked two by two to the beach each

day wearing a bathing costume and bee shirt with new sandals, which hurt a bit, but never mind, we were seeing the beach for the first time. Each of us boys had our own bucket and spade which we showed off proudly. I couldn't swim in those days, but I somehow reached Winkle Island, where I filled my bucket up with these snail like creatures.

The Sisters washed and boiled the winkles and with a blunt pin we picked them out of their shells. They were lovely and luxurious as we sat on the stony beach. I remember the Sisters would stop us eating the winkles

43

until the afternoon, or we wouldn't eat our dinner, which we found far less interesting.

The view of Littlehampton in those days was of the large big dipper and the funfair. We were treated very liberally to a few rides, and I particularly remember the bumper cars and the slide, although we had to be very careful, for there was very little money in those days, and we certainly didn't get any pocket money. For two days we were unable to go to the beach as it rained and rained. Even our extra prayers were not being answered, and Sister Veronica asked us to pray louder so Jesus could hear:

"Please God, let the sun out today, and let it stop raining!"

Sister Veronica then had a wonderful idea and disappeared to make a telephone call. On her return all she would tell us was that we had a surprise to look forward to, 'so get your raincoats on, we are going to walk the half mile to Littlehampton town centre.' Two by two we marched to the

44

centre, stopping outside the cinema. Sister had called them and asked if she could have 30 free seats for 30 little boys who came from a boys home! They happily agreed, and even bought us ice creams. The film we saw starred Diana Dors, then all the rage, along with David Kossoff. The name of the film was 'A Kid For Two Farthings', which we all sat and watched with the thoughtful and kind Sisters; a perfect end to the best two weeks of my life.

After my holidays in tender Littlehampton, I moved to the larger boys' home in Enfield, and what luck; during our summer holidays we went to St Mary's bay, which was in Dymchurch, Kent. The coaches from St Joseph's were different; they were cream and brown in colour, and a little scruffier. Sister would ask

The boys outside 'Sheffield' hut.

us all to close our eyes and put your hands together, where we would selfishly pray for good weather. It's funny how sincere we

all were in front of all these selfish bigger boys, everybody could hear our prayers.

Before we set off Sister asked if there were any boys that suffered from coach sickness. for in the front seats were lots of coloured plastic buckets that were to be handed to the 'sickdirts'. There was only one on our coach whose name I can't remember but I'm sure he was one of the boys who used to visit with his mum for tea at Pearson's.

The beach was stony, but when the tide went out you were left with miles, or so it seemed, of sand where we often used to play cricket and footy of course, or perhaps a game of five stones.

The greatest treat was to receive our daily spending money, which I wasted going to my first ever grown up cafe. I ordered double egg and chips with watered down tomato sauce all for 11 pence including a drink; my favourite being an apple drink called 'Cidrax'. Egg and chips never tasted so yum yummish!

In the corner of the cafe was the latest juke box, it was very popular; all the boys and girls took turns to put a shilling in

Boys at play on the beach at St Mary's Bay.

the slot and we would listen to the hits of the '50s. Remember, skiffle was king; we would hear Lonnie Donegan singing 'Putting on the Style', Johnny Duncan and his Blue Grass Boys catching 'The Last Train to San Fernando', and of course Don Lang and his Frantic Five with 'School Days'. Another name that springs to mind from those days is Terry Dene, with his song 'A White Sports Coat and a Pink Carnation', but my favourite skiffle song was the great Lonnie Donegan vehicle, 'Cumberland Gap'.

18348   JEFFERSTONE LANE, ST. MARY'S BAY.

Although all the other boys enjoyed swimming at the sandy beach, it was that cafe with its double egg and chips that really thrilled me, and if you could afford it, for an extra two pence they would even put a sausage on the plate, with a slice of bread and marg! Music and entertainment had also become a part of camp life. One of the men helpers by the name of Hugh Maynard introduced music into the dorms and was also in charge of film shows, together with Toc. H (a charity which brought the magic of the cinema into the boys' home). It was not all skiffle; one of the musical hits of my seaside remembrances was 'High Noon', or as it is more commonly known: 'Do not Forsake me oh my Darling on this our Wedding Day', sung by Tex Ritter. The other big hit in the dorm to wake us up was 'I'll be Home my Darling, Please Wait for me', by Pat Boone.

The entertainment would take many forms and I was asked on the last day of one holiday if I wanted to box one of the Barnardo boys to a 'living hell'. I never much liked the bigger boys from Dr Barnardo's, tough louts, but in spite of this I was persuaded to be a punch bag for three two minute rounds. I was knocked around and given a dose of a bloody nose, but strangely enough I danced away from real trouble, keeping clear from the punches of this Barnardo lout as best I could. Of course, I lost. There was muted applause as my opponents hand was raised in victory, then the referee lifted my hand sky high, and it was to be the loser who got the biggest roar of the day. Afterwards I spoke to Les Parsons, one of the men helpers, and asked why he had encouraged me, knowing full well that boxing was not my thing and that I was scared to fight? He said:

"I knew you would be a dignified loser, and everybody likes a brave loser. Paul, you were absolutely right to represent Joey's. I say to you, use your hands carefully and don't murder the living daylights out of anybody, not that you could."

Thank you Les, I shall stick to draughts and tiddlywinks.

ST. MARY'S BAY HOLIDAY CAMP C

The holidays I spent firstly in Littlehampton and then in the army huts at St Mary's Bay were truly memorable and exciting to a young boy. What more could you want? There is, however, one holiday memory from my childhood which stands out as both strange and wonderful:

The Secret of Winkle Island, Littlehampton.

I was 10 years old and this was to be the very last day of my holiday to Littlehampton. I had been to Littlehampton many times as a small boy and I had got used to the routine set up by the Sisters but this day was different. It was a glorious sunny, warm day that I shall remember all my life. After breakfast the thirty boys would slowly walk two by two, crocodile style to the sand and stony beach where we would spend the day splashing each other, shrieking, giggling and laughing, with the Sisters keeping a close eye.

Sister Veronica would lead the boys and Sister Vincent would make sure that the stragglers at the back would keep up, but this was a special day, and the Sisters realizing that the sun would burn our small bodies, used calamine lotion as suncream.

Although we had been to the beach many times, we were greeted for the first time by a very low tide. We had never realized that the beach was so sandy as it stretched out into the distance; I could only see the sea on the horizon. As the weather was perfect the Sisters suggested that we had our picnic on the bright,sandy beach. Laying in the sun I found it strange that I could see Littlehampton very differently from any other time that I could remember, a clear blue sky, very warm and a perfect day to spend hours on the beach.

Our buckets and spades were used in all the ways that we could dream up, but I had winkles on my mind, and so with my friend David Heafy for the first time we walked, not waded to winkle island which was usually hidden by the salty sea. We began in earnest to fill our buckets up with the winkles, which tasted so delicious and were free, other than the time spent picking them from the large, seaweed covered rocks. We could see clearly for the first time the whole island, it was winkle paradise.

David and I were lost in our own world and did not hear the many cries from the Sisters to say that the tide was coming in quickly and would soon take back the stony beach. David was two months older than me, and was a little taller, so I handed him the bucket of winkles and removed my new sandals which I was keen to look after. I asked that he hand them to the Sisters for safekeeping when he reached the shore as I wanted to carry on picking winkles and had not realised the danger. The Sisters and the boys were shouting:

"COME ON OUT PAULIE, THE WATER WILL COVER YOU VERY SOON... YOU CAN'T SWIM!"

David could float and dive and was a stylish swimmer. How I envied him, for I was afraid of the salty water. He waded back with difficulty as the tide rose, carrying the goodies. He handed them to the two anxious Sisters who asked him to go back and get me off the island, for they were afraid I would drown. David couldn't swim out quickly enough to help me. I was becoming increasingly fearful and decided to make for the shore, but by this time the water was coming in quickly and it was too late. I turned for the last time to see winkle island covered over with sea water, I slipped and went under, I had no time to call for help, how do you know you are drowning?

I must have been under the water for no more than ten seconds, and then the miracle occurred, my small body floated to the top, I opened my eyes, staring at the sky, drops of water running from my face. Who taught me how to float? I wasn't taking gulps of salt water and for the first time ever I was happy to be in the sea. I remembered how David could swim so I nervously splashed my legs, and copied his actions. By that time David had arrived and realised there was no longer any danger. He and I splashed around, floated, shouted as I moved my body about in a way which I suppose was swimming. But how could I do all these things when I was so afraid of the water? The Sisters were by this time frantic, still shouting 'Come on out!' At last we both come out of the water, grinning like mad. The Sisters were so releived and forgave us immediately. We dried off quickly, put on our beach clothes and returned back to Seaford house, crocodile style, what a day. At the time I remember thinking 'this is the best day of my life'.

Epilogue.

We were in bed early, and both David and I were very tired and very happy. Paulie at last could swim. David and I had beds next to each other, so we talked the night away. Sister Veronica turned the lights off saying;

"Get a good nights sleep, for tomorrow at 9 o'clock, the coach will be waiting to take us back to St. Vincent's, join your hands, close your eyes and say your goodnight prayers; an Our Father, a Hail Mary, and a Glory be."

The other boys were sleeping the night away, but I was still awake and full of excitement. Sister shone the torch on each boy, there were thirty of us, and I was the last one. She came over and leaned over my bed and said:

"I thought you had drowned, that's why I had sent your friend David in, to perhaps help you should you get into difficulty. I remember how afraid you were of the water and I knew you couldn't swim. Paulie, remember, never do that again, you frightened the life out of me."

I promised, and my eyes were slowly giving way to a peaceful, dreamy sleep. I opened my eyes and noticed that Sister Veronica had a tear in her eye.

"Sleep well Paulie." she whispered.

Mr Smith the Woodwork Teacher.

Mr Smith, the woodwork teacher, blew his whistle and all playtime noise would stop. He blew the second time; we all quietly walked into our year group. The third whistle went; we would all march two by two, returning to our classroom. Suddenly we heard a noisy aeroplane over head.

"It's alright, it's one of ours." I said to my best friend Frank McGrath.

"Who said that?"

"I did Mr Smith."

"You and McGrath stay there, don't move an inch!"

We watched as the boys and girls marched into their respective rooms. Somehow, alone, just standing there, the playground seemed very big and frightening. We stood there for what felt like an hour before the woodwork teacher, Mr Smith, came out holding a cane in his large, fat hands. He looked at me, up and down, then returned to the classroom to get the appropriate size cane for my height, as I was small. He came slowly towards us, Frank began to cry. I looked at him and said,

"Frank no, please, no..." his tears were unstoppable.

Schoolboy, age 13.

57

Mr Smith just looked at him and said:

"Get out of my sight.... You stay here Delrue. What did I tell you Delrue, about speaking after I blew the whistle? All noise was to stop, got it? But you continued talking."

"But Mr Smith, I had only said what you have said many times as an aeroplane came overhead: It's alright, it's one of ours!" I replied.

"Get your hand out, straight out, straight out!"

I curled my fingers inwards so as to protect myself. He noticed, and with the cane he re-opened the palm of my hand. He held the cane high and came crashing down onto my small hands. The playground echoed with the sound.

"Get the other hand out, straight, remember!!"

I held my hand out straight as a dye. He held the cane high

over his head and again, with all his might came crashing down. It really hurt, I was numb with pain, but he did not make me cry, he would never do that, he would never win...

"Get your hand out again."

I did as I was told. I never felt a thing, my hands were too numb.

"Mr Smith, did I get the other two canings for Frank?"

He just looked at me, I had never seen such anger on his face. He went white. He threw everything at me, caned me all over and could not stop such was his rage. I put my hands over my face, he pulled me down still hitting me all over my body. He fell on top of me, his sweat poured all over me.

"Mr Smith, stop this immediately! Stop this at once! Leave the boy alone!"

The headmaster Mr Martin had seen all from his office window and rushed out to take the cane from a heavy breathing Mr Smith.

"Come into my Office!" Mr Martin shouted.

"It's the last time for you... Delrue, go to your classroom."

I slowly got up from the ground and walked away, as upright as I could manage. I felt hot all over and was in great pain, but I held my pride and did not cry. By this time all the kids were looking out of the school windows, such was the commotion. Before I went back into the class I stopped at the toilets and put my head under the cold water tap. I looked into the mirror and saw my face for the first time, red and

'When I'm crying, when all seems lost, Remember, there will be another time.'

sweaty. I slowly took my school shirt off, then my vest. My body was marked badly; cane marks from my chest across to my back. Bruised all over. It was then that I wept and wept. Part of my back was bleeding. I was stunned, shaking; my small body had taken Mr Smiths brutal caning. I put my hands under the cold tap, the weight of the water hurt, such was the bruising, my right hand seemed larger than the left, and my thumb nail was ripped out. A kid asked if I was alright. I turned around.

"Is there anything I can do?"

I looked at him and cried, with my arms over his shoulders I held him tight. It was minutes before I let go. He helped me put on my vest and shirt and helped me back to class. Before I entered the classroom I stopped for a moment. I asked that he never tell a living soul that I had cried. He kept his word. As for my best friend Frank; we were never the same, we stayed friends but we never spoke of my beating with Mr Smith the woodwork teacher. We were distant when we left school and I never saw him again. He went to live with his mother at 66 Church Road, Willesden.

I did receive, out of the blue, many years later a letter from the boy who held my hand at my lowest school moment. He told me how much that incident had affected him and how he had cried for me in his bedroom that night. He still thinks it was the bravest moment he has seen in his life, but that he had broken his promise and told his children of the time he saw me break down and cry. I was only a school boy of 13 years. I saw life differently. I became afraid of grown ups, but always I looked up and saw that the moon was yellow and not red after all.

Paul and Frank

'At school we were always
keen to be led astray.'

I will Never Find my way Home.

My sister Simone came for me and brought me to Putney. I was to stay for my first ever weekend with my real family. It was a strange atmosphere, whispers, nothing prepared for my stay. I was to sleep in the T.V. room, which was at the front of the house. The family had planned nothing. I was to get used to living at home, a family home. I was afraid and said little, just politeness. What would it be like when I reached fifteen years and had to stay there for ever, could I ever cope? London seemed very unfriendly and big. I was cold and worried.

Piccadilly Circus.

I had to return to the boys' home at Enfield on my own. I had never travelled in London on my own and the weekend was full of worries. One of the memorable little cruelties of that weekend was that I had no money and my mother knew it. I had to steal the fare back to Enfield from my mother's handbag and in her purse there was only half a crown, just the right amount. I was too afraid to ask her or my stepfather George for the fare. I never had money of my own. The home gave me just enough money for a one way ticket. It was dark when I left Putney to return home to Enfield, on my own. I walked up Kevil Drive, toward Putney Hill, to wait for the number 14 bus, which would take me to King's Cross.

I waited for half an hour before somebody told me that the number 14 bus does not run on a Sunday, so, I walked down Putney Hill towards the town and was told by a friendly bus conductor that a number 30 bus would get me to King's Cross. Anxieties grew, I had never travelled by bus in the dark and I did not know where King's Cross was. I was terrified; I kept looking out of the steamed up window for a sign: 'King's Cross'.

'I long for peace of mind, and that nobody can give.'

The bus went through Putney Town, towards Fulham, then South Kensington, onto Hyde Park, and onwards to Piccadilly. I was in a dream, a dark dream, hot and sweaty. I began to suffer from bus sickness, will the bus ever stop at King's Cross, had I missed the stop? The lights and advertising boards where all I saw. I looked at my watch, an hour was nearly up, but there was no sign for King's Cross. The conductor came towards me, he could see I was troubled and said:

"King's Cross is the next stop."

I dinged the bell and got off the bus with my small brown carrier bag, holding my change of weekend clothes. This was King's Cross but where was the railway station that would take me back to the boys' home? I will never find my way home. I was

Holtswhites Hill, returning home at dusk.

afraid of asking people. It took me many worried hours walking around until a Policeman held my hand and took me to King's Cross Railway Station ticket office. I felt for the money in my coat pocket, but I had lost it. I started to cry. The policeman asked the ticket man to give the boy a single ticket to Enfield, and then paid the fare. He smiled and still holding my hand took me to the platform and train for Enfield. He opened the train door and I got in.

It was now quite dark but I noticed his kindly smile as the train left quietly for my real home, my home for 15 years in Enfield. I walked up Holtwhites Hill towards St Joseph's where I was met by Sister Joseph who asked me if I enjoyed my first and only weekend with my family in London. I just looked at her, smiled and said I felt very tired. It was 10.30pm, way past my bedtime. Sister walked me slowly to the dorm, helped me undress and tucked me in to the warmth and security of my familiar bed, where I dreamed the night away. I have never forgotten my first journey home. At last, I had found my way home.

My real home.

St Joseph's Boys' Home.

Having Tea at Pearson's Department Store.

The warmth and security of St Vincent's Boys' Home ended when I was 11 years old in 1955 when I was sent to live at the much larger home in Enfield called St Joseph's. Being amongst bigger boys made me unhappy and the teachers there often caned me, for no good reason.

Like all the other kids, I looked forward to Saturdays when we collected our weekly nine pence pocket money. I earned an extra sixpence because I cleaned the upstairs dormitory lavatory. It was a dirty job and no-one was keen to take it on, but I remember walking into the lav carrying a bucket of water, a scrubbing brush, a wooden scraper and a tin of Gumption, holding my breath. For three months I cleaned that lav before handing over to another brave soul.

In my second year on the top floor, I was mostly happy in my dorm and friendly with the other boys, especially David Rutter, the boy with the mountainous quiff. He had a small side locker holding Brylcreem and an album with foreign stamps which got kicked in to get at its contents; David never seemed to get angry on these occasions and stayed calm.

I was slight, blue-eyed and fair haired, quiet and thoughtful. I was rarely bullied, unlike some of the smaller kids but I never seemed to make close friendships, as I had done at St Vincent's. I was at Feltham for eleven years and Enfield for four, before leaving to live with my mother and her family in Putney. I lived there for three unhappy years, working in a leather factory at King's Cross.

Now, back to my story or perhaps an impression. I've always been good at telling stories but this one is mostly true:

It was an early June day, warm and sunny, as I walked down Holtwhites Hill towards Enfield town centre, planning to bunk into the Rialto flick house to see the latest cowboy film. The Rialto was the easiest cinema to bunk into, as the lavatory window looked over Enfield Town market. Because I was slim and agile

The Rialto Cinema, Enfield Square.

I could easily climb the low wall, squeeze in through the small window and onto the lavatory seat to wait for the cinema lights to dim. Then I would open the back door quietly, to let the other kids in, reminding them to sit next to adults if the film was an 'A', pretending that you were with your Mum and Dad. But on this Saturday something happened to make me feel sad and thoughtful. As I collected my pocket money from Sister Joseph, I saw along the hallway a kid in school uniform and a lady in a light grey suit, wearing a simple, smart hat. I could only see her back but recognised David, who smiled at me. The lady turned and gave me a warm kindly smile as well; it was his mother. I hurried along towards town with the other kids but something was on my mind.

"Paul, hurry up, the flicks start at 2 o'clock!" someone shouted.

I hardly heard what they were saying as they began to run towards the Rialto cinema. Instead, I crossed the busy road to Pearson's Department Store. It was the largest store in Enfield selling just about everything a small boy would have no interest in, windows full of outfits for ladies and gentlemen, everything for the modern, colourful kitchen, fur coats, the latest radios and Ferguson black and white televisions, the very latest models. Being truly bored by the windows I headed back to the large, glass entrance doors with

'I never saw him so happy and so free from care.'

the large brass handles, loitering for a few minutes before bravely venturing into this posh shop, for the first time.

"Can I help you? Well, what do you want? I haven't got all day, I have work to do. What do you want?"

A tall lady appeared at my side, making me aware of how dirty and scruffy I looked in my play clothes. I tried to smooth my hair to look more presentable but she looked quick tempered and unfriendly as I mumbled to her that I had arranged to meet my mother there, for Tea at three o'clock.

"Well, why didn't you say so, in the first place?! And mind out of the way of the other customers!" she snapped.

Pulling at my grey socks, I realised what a sad lot I looked as she continued, commenting that it was after three already and that she would be keeping her eye on me. From her glass office in the centre of the shop, I could see her picking up the telephone and speaking rapidly as she stared at me; I made a dash for the stairs.

As I ran into Pearson's Tea Rooms on the first floor, a young woman in white, with a little red hat asked if she could help me as

I "seemed a little lost". She smiled kindly and offered to seat me, and I explained I was there to meet my mother, who was a little late.

"I'm sure she will be here any minute." she said as she moved off to serve her customers.

Sitting there I let my eyes wander from table to table, watching the lady in white bringing plates of finely cut sandwiches to her customers, pouring tea from an attractive white tea pot, whilst they added milk and sugar-lumps to their china cups. The couple on the next table were having soup with bread and butter, but most were eating sandwiches and talking in whispers. How I wished I could join them, eating so daintily.

Apart, from the tables for two, was a larger table with a family seated at it; they were making so much noise and laughter that I longed to be invited over. The children seemed so comfortable and happy, clean and smartly dressed like their mum and dad. They saw me, in my play clothes, waiting for my mother: I felt very ashamed with my dirty knees and face and tried to smooth my unruly fringe, but it was no good, I felt out of place and uncomfortable, although I managed to smile back at them.

The sad feelings of being alone would not go, despite the fact that in my pocket was the nine pence pocket money and the extra tanner from cleaning the lav. I watched the nice lady in white as she passed around glass dishes of butter and jam for the scones and teacakes from table to table. Her hair was mostly covered by the red hat, apart from a friendly fringe that bobbed as she passed by. She smiled, perhaps a little sorry that my mother had not turned up, perhaps guessing that I had made the story up. Waiting there I felt very alone, watching the ladies in flowery dresses and smart hats accompanied by gentlemen in suits and sports jackets, elegantly buttering their scones and applying smooth, even layers of jam. It seemed so posh to me and I felt very out of place.

More food appeared, my eyes following the plates of cakes served from the trolley. I was so hungry, my mouth watered and

I wiped the moisture away with my fingers as unobtrusively as I could. Then, out of the corner of my eye, I spotted familiar faces; David Rutter and his elegant mother in grey, still wearing the neat, attractive hat that flattered her small, long face. She wore little make-up, just a touch of powder and lipstick. I just gazed at David and his mum, so happy together, pouring tea, passing sandwiches and cake and exchanging smiles. David ate so elegantly, looking smart in his uniform and with his Brylcreemed quiff, it made me feel scruffier than ever.

They seemed so at ease as they talked to each other. I knew David was due to be leaving St Joseph's in a few months time and I imagined them planning their first ever home together. I was sure they would live in a really nice house with a dog for a family pet and perhaps David might meet his grandparents and dad, the dad he never talked about to me. My father had been killed in the war, parachuting over France, a very brave man I thought. I didn't even know what he had looked like. Twenty-one years old and very brave, the Sisters had said.

I was daydreaming away, when the nice lady in white said softly that she did not think my mother was coming to have tea with me after all.

"I'm so sorry. What's your name?" she said.

"Paul Delrue." I replied.

"Where do you really live?" she asked, gently.

I thought hard and long before telling her that I lived at St Joseph's Boys' Home, a mile away on Holtwhites Hill.

"I've heard of it." she said

"And I've seen lots of the kids walking in the High Street. I've only been working here for a few months and I don't want to lose my job talking to you, but I do understand you. My own husband was killed in the war, leaving me with three boys of my own. My sister helps me to care for them. The youngest one is called Paul too, after his father. You remind me of my own boy, fair and sensitive with a happy face that sometimes seems so sad. Now, I've put three cream cakes aside for myself but I'm going to give them to you. They are in this bag; put them under your jumper and be careful not to squeeze them! You must go now, or I'll lose my job but I'd be so happy to see you again, sometime."

The New River, Enfield.

She gave me the most understanding of smiles, before turning away to her customers again.

As I walked down the stairs and out of Pearson's clutching my small parcel of cream cakes, I was anxious not to meet the hateful woman I had spoken to earlier. She was still talking on the telephone in her glass office. I left the shop and broke into a run as I crossed the road leading to the Rialto Cinema. I carried on past the market place to the New River, my favourite walk.

There, I could be alone with my thoughts of the warm, kind lady I wished could have been my mother, with a son called Paul, who I was sure was her favourite. I scoffed the cakes (which were out of this world) making them last as long as possible and licked the cream slowly from around my dirty face. I didn't care.

Slowly, I walked back to St Joseph's, just in time for supper. Saturday Tea was usually the best, with bloater paste sandwiches and chocolate spread, followed by fruit or seed cake all washed down with urn-tea. The tea was smoky and awful, but I got used to it, swallowing it in quick gulps. This night, because of my cream cakes, I did not feel very hungry but a gnawing feeling inside me made me feel very sad.

I tried to remind myself of all the things the other kids liked about me, my cheerfulness, light and smiling, the fact that I was a good bunker-in and could nick fags for my older friends, despite hating the smell of the things. They paid me back in boiled sweets and it made me popular.

Deep in thought, I sat in my usual chair. David Rutter came in, smiling and happy. He sat next to me:

"How did it go? How many kids did you bunk in? Was it a good cowboy film?"

I asked David to excuse me, walking quickly out of the dining room to the playground. The kids were kicking a ball around, passing it to one another, shooting for goal and pestering me to join in. It was all too much and I ran off at speed to the dykes, where I knew I could be alone. I opened the door of the sit-ons and sat down on the wooden pan seat with my head in my hands. Minutes passed and I began to cry. Why did I feel this way? Think, Delrue, think!

*'He knew, he realized.
I was human and sad,
A person, a someone,
I was so glad.'*

"What's up, Paulie, why are you crying? You never cry. Can I help?"

It was Tony Kavanagh, slowly opening the door and witnessing me shedding tears I did not wish to hide.

"I don't know what she looks like, I can't see her."

As Tony helped me wipe away my tears, he asked me who I was talking about.

"I can't remember what my mother's face looks like. I've been at St Joseph's for nearly four years and she's never been to see me since I last saw her at St Vincent's a long, long time ago. Does your Mum ever visit you, Tony?"

"Yes, once a year she always takes me out for tea at Pearson's on the High Street. But I do miss her and wonder if she will come for me when I leave Joey's next summer, like you do. We'll always be friends, always be together." Tony said, as he passed me his shirt sleeve to wipe away my tears.

I smiled my usual smile as we walked out of the dykes and into the playground.

The boys of St Joseph's with Dick Quinton (centre).

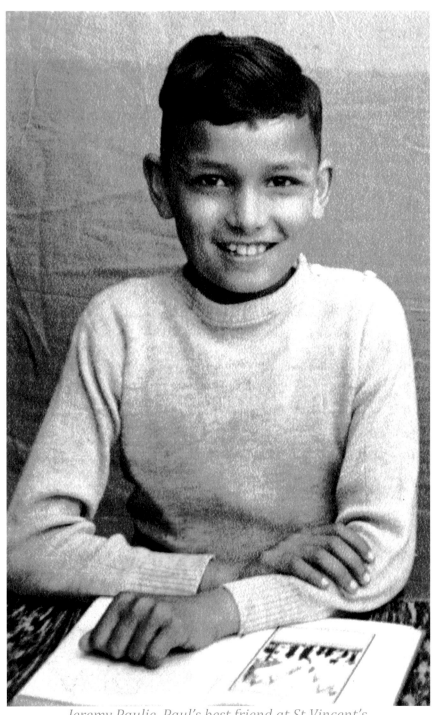

Jeremy Paulie, Paul's best friend at St Vincent's.

Old Times.

Frank McGrath liked Madeira cake, I always preferred fruit cake.

Stephen Timlin gave me my first good hiding and I still have the scars, look closely at my lips.

John Grange and I played 'What's my Line'. I was always better and guessed much easier. It's funny; I have not seen him for years. We met at St Vincent's Boys' Home, way back in the 1950's. I last saw him in 1954, just before I left Feltham to live in Enfield, again another boys' home.

My friend was Eddie Satterthwaite, he was tall and fair, with a kind understanding – how he saved my neck many times. I remember clearly how he took the blame when Humpy Wright caught me in the Orchard nicking apples. Humpy would cycle to St Joseph's up Holtwhites Hill each day and was feared by all.

It was in St Vincent's Boys' Home that I befriended three kids that gave me a special feeling of true friendship Somehow, all these years later I still maintain special feelings, a kind of warmth and inner understanding with these three boys; Jeremy Paulie, Terance Quinn and Lawrence Gaforg. We were always on each others side.

Their faces are still as clear and their names never forgotten, I wonder if they ever feel the same for me. It would be wonderful to meet again but then, perhaps not. Growing up is always a disappointment and you lose so much.

No, let me keep my three friends alive and young just as I remember, it is really better that way.

74

'I shall grow my garden, and cultivate my friends.'

A White Bag of Peaches.

I left St Joseph's Boys' Home in the summer of 1959 to live in Putney, London. I moved into a shared house of three families and an old lady, Mrs Bessent, who lived on the ground floor. We, as a family lived on the first floor. I shared a bedroom with my seventeen year old sister Simone; living with my mother, stepfather George and young brother Norman. Although my sister and I had the surname Delrue, my family were known as the Stephens. As for me I felt different from the start. I had just turned fifteen years and it was the first time I had lived in London, travelling each morning to the leather factory in King's Cross.

At first I travelled to work by the number 14 bus, then, once I had got used to the underground I would walk to East Putney railway station, catching the train and travelling half fare, for I looked like a very young fifteen year old. It would cost me two shillings a day, return. My first week's wages were three pounds 10 shillings. I thought it was a fortune. My wages soon went up to four pounds a week, of which my mother asked for two pounds 10 shillings. This I dutifully gave her, leaving the money on the kitchen sill every Friday. I never missed a week all the time I lived there. I had to fend for myself for the first time and I found it difficult sometimes to live on the remaining one pound 10 shillings, from which I would pay for my journey by train to King's Cross each day. I would have to be at work by eight,

clock on and walk up to the fourth floor, where I would work in the pattern department until 5.30, with a half hour off for lunch. I took meat paste sandwiches and was kindly given food by the old men who also worked in the leather factory. The work was routine but I quite enjoyed it. I was well liked, polite and well mannered, but more importantly I was always on time, tidy and eager to work. I stayed at the factory in King's Cross for a year and a half, leaving to become an apprentice bookbinder for University College, still in London, not far from the Leather Factory.

The only friend I had was a boy who grew up with me at St Vincent's Boys' Home, his name was Ian Macgregor. I had known him since I was five; he was a couple of years older, taller, bigger built, with a mop of wavy golden hair. He was fun to be with. We liked each other and tidied up the school room each day, eating the leftovers after the teachers had finished and gone home. How we looked

Ian MacGregor.

forward to the real bread and butter, plain biscuits and sugar lumps. Ian remained my only friend during my time in Putney. I would cycle to his home in Hampton Wick (near Kingston Upon Thames) quite often. We would cycle to Brighton during warm sunny weekends in the summer, for Ian had an old aunt who lived in the poorest part of old Brighton. We would stay a couple of nights and return to our homes in Putney and Hampton Wick. We were very close friends and furthermore he drove a bread van for a living, a super job. He was real smart, with a white uniform and a small baseball hat over his golden curls. He smiled a lot and loved his job, travelling each day to Fulham, Hammersmith, Shepherd's Bush and Harlsden.

Ryegate Hill.

It was Ian who suggested I saved up for a push bike for the daily journey to King's Cross. So I saved up the great sum in those days of £13 – for a Hampton Wick push bike. I was on my way. I left home at 6.45 am; push biked through London to be at the Leather Factory at King's Cross by 7.55 am. I continued to ride my bike when I left the factory for my new job at University College in Gower Street. I enjoyed the freedom it gave me to travel the seven miles to the bindery each day, although Putney Hill was a bit scary. I enjoyed passing the London Theatres in Piccadilly and Shaftsbury Avenue. My favourite singer Anthony Newley was in a show at 'The Queen's' called 'Stop the World I Want to Get Off'. I saw the show with the forwarder Reg Denham and loved it. It was the very first time I had ever been to the theatre. I went to the theatre with Reg many times after that. I caught the theatre bug, seeing 'My Fair Lady', 'The Music Man' and Sammy Davies at the London Palladium. It only stopped when I moved to Leagrave, Bedfordshire two years later.

I was still living at home with my family. Life for me was strained and difficult. I was rarely spoken to and certainly not cared for. It was always so very cold, and sharing a bedroom with my sister Simone, I was never able to do the natural things that young teenagers grow into. But I had the spring and the summer to look forward to; to push bike through London Town in bright early mornings was my biggest thrill. It was late summer when my mother told me I had to leave Putney and stay for three weeks with my grandma Violette in Chiswick, while she went on her caravan holiday to Dorset with her husband George and my smaller brother Norman. I had visited Chiswick a few times by train but never by bike. I was not looking forward to it. To be with further family grown ups put fear into me; how should I behave, how will I be greeted? My friend Reg told me how to get there on push bike; to travel to Edgware Road, the Queensway onto Goldhawk Road then finally Chiswick, Number 6 Netheravon Road to be met by my Gran, who I was told should be addressed as 'Auntie Violette'.

'I am warm but can not reach the sun.'

Auntie Violette's house was attractive and quite large, with an openness about it; it glowed. Unlike Putney, it was well attended and looked after. It had three floors and I had the airy top bedroom to myself. I had never had a bedroom to myself. It seems I was in heaven for the first time. I was warmly greeted

The programme; a shilling.

and shown to my room, passing the kitchen on the second floor which smelled unlike anything I had ever smelled before. Walking up those stairs I could almost taste the magic herbs and things. It smelled like a French home, for my Grandfather Charles (who had died two years earlier) was some kind of special cook and had passed on his food skills to this his third wife, who I was to call Auntie Violette. She was an elegant lady, tall and slim with greying curly hair, a kind face and a full warm smile that I loved. She was beautifully dressed, always attractive and tasteful, a real classy act with bright blue sad eyes that seemed to express a lot of hurt. I wonder if like me, she was not accepted by the family, perhaps she felt the same, an outsider, but she, like me, never let on.

I knew for three whole weeks I was going to be perfectly happy. I looked around in my new nicely papered bedroom in which you could swing a thousand cats. A big bedroom all of my own. I slowly changed from my push bike clothes into something more comfortable, laying them across the bed neatly. I could not believe it! I followed the kitchen smell downstairs. Auntie was busy getting the evening meal ready when she pointed to a white bag on the kitchen table.

"Paul, Simone told me you liked Peaches, so when I went to Sanders the fruit shop I bought you a bag of three. They're all for you, if you want you can take them to work."

I looked down at the kitchen table seeing

6 Netheravon Road, Chiswick.

the white bag, my Auntie was smiling at me. I was suddenly overwhelmed, and leaving the kitchen I walked slowly up to my bedroom. I threw myself onto the bed crying heavy tears, silent and uncontrollable. I turned, looking up to the ceiling, the tears were rolling down my cheeks onto the soft blankets. It was the first ever act of kindness any member of my family had shown me. I was so overwhelmed, I stayed in my room until I recovered. I went down to the kitchen where Auntie Violette had put out the evening meal, which smelled beautiful and was cooked to perfection. There were homemade sausages, creamed potatoes, seasoned and fresh green beans, all with a tasty white sauce. After I had finished I looked at the white bag, slowly took out a peach, smiled and had my first bite. It tasted as though it had come from the Garden of Eden. Auntie could tell I had cried but said nothing. Her kindness meant more to me than I could express. As a child growing up, I remember the white bag of peaches as the first act of family kindness to me.

My three weeks living with my Auntie were the best ever. I loved travelling to 6 Netheravon Road and my Uncle Paul often joined us, he was nice and always pleased to see me. We got to know each other well during those few weeks, we would walk together getting shopping, newspapers, having tea at his local cafe. He tried telling me the history of our family. He spoke of how, with my mother he had visited me when I was 13 at St Vincent's Boys' Home in Feltham. Uncle Paul had lived with Auntie Violette since Grandpa Charles had died two years ago. He helped around the house and garden and was really kind to me, often cooking me meals, talking to me with trust in his voice, I think I took a shine to him. He had so much personality and was always fun to be with.

As for me, I was introverted, shy, rather frightened, neat, well mannered and I kept my feelings mostly to myself. I never let on I was unhappy living with my mother in Putney, but I honestly think they knew. The three weeks in Chiswick went by very quickly and I returned to an unloving house. I never told them that I felt happiness for the first time with my Uncle Paul and my Auntie Violette. Many years later, when I had a family of my own I named my first borne after her. As for Ian, my friend from St Vincent's Boys' Home, he died three years ago, my best boyhood friend. In these few leaves I honour his memory, a boy with golden wavy hair who was always making motor bike noises.

He's like me at Fifteen.

"He's like me at fifteen; small, neat and nobody notices."

I walk towards East Putney underground railway station and collect my ticket like everyone else. The railways doors slide open, then close and I sit in a corner next to the window. The train stops at the next station, a crowd enters, no one sits next to me. They get out their newspapers and cigarettes, familiar and all alike. Slowly the train enters the next station, Parsons Green, this time just a few people enter. Still no one sits next to me. I only have two more stops to go, the train is beginning to smell of early morning sweating bodies. The train stops to open the doors, one boy gets on, he looks at me, sits next to me, he brushes against me as he sits down, making himself comfortable. We look at each other through the reflection of the opposite window, as it enters into the dark tunnel we smile at each other. The sliding doors open and close, the train goes on its way to Earl's Court, my station. The doors open and I fight my way out, leaving the boy alone. The door closes and the train leaves. I look to see the boy, he looks like me, nobody is sitting next to him, the train is quite full and moves on its way to Kensington High Street............ slowly.

Two Fat Ladies.

It was on the last sunny Saturday of July 1959 that I said goodbye to St Joseph's Boys' Home in Enfield, my home for 4 years. I was not as happy as I had been at St Vincent's; I never made close friends at Enfield. In my last school years at St George's Roman Catholic School I was very afraid of the teachers and my learning skills suffered. I was always comfortable with English, painting and P.T. I was teacher's favourite at sport, running, dancing to music and singing. I loathed woodwork with Mr Smith but he was a fine teacher, particularly at painting and he got the best out of me with English lessons and story telling. I loved compositions; I read my compositions out to my fellow boy students who were amazed at my 'making up'. It became easy to me, I lived in a world of fantasy.

Sister Joseph bade me farewell, my mother, stepfather and young brother Norman came for me in their motorbike and sidecar, a B.S.A. I was to learn afterwards. My mother never came in for me, and neither did stepfather George. It was just the noise of the motorbike that drew the attention of the Sisters. I walked slowly down the large white steps, turning around to Sister. I had tears in my eyes, but never let on. I climbed onto George's bike, holding him tight and we were off. I was sad at leaving St Joseph's, my home since I was a babe in arms, looked after by the Crusade of Rescue and given pastoral care by the Sisters of Charity. I was not ready (in the same way as most of the kids) to leave the home with all it's safety, and go out into an unfriendly world. I travelled to Putney in fear, knowing nothing except how to play football and games. I was used to boys, not grown-ups and worst of all family; a thing I did not understand and was never to really know.

I slide off the back of the bike slowly and look up at the faded Victorian house I was to call home for three years. Three most unhappy years that were to affect my whole outlook. I was to know and feel the unfairness of life and learn that grown-ups were not to be trusted. I never felt a mother's love, I was never wanted. I was in the way, I was an embarrassment, but they had to take me from the home after fifteen years. You had to leave and be friendless, all the friends I had were left behind at St Joseph's. My mother said to me:

"Is that all you have, just one carrier bag?"

I did not answer.

"What do you have in the bag?"

"Clothes." I replied, (a pair of linings, a woolly vest a pair of new grey long trousers, school shirt and tie, pyjamas, and a small pair of school grey socks).

"Will the rest of your clothes be sent on?"

"There is no rest, this is all I was given, like the rest of the boys."

The house at 2 Holmbush Road, Putney seemed sadly neglected. The ground floor was home to the Wakefield's along with old Mrs Bessant, the Stephens's; my family (for I was given my mother's maiden name) were on the middle floor with the extra bedroom. I was to share a bedroom with my sister Simone, who was seventeen years old. On the top floor were the Pearson's, they had two children and one of them, John Pearson was the same age as me.

My mother was on good terms with everyone, (outwardly at least) friendly and well loved. She seemed always to attract friendly faces around her. I could not understand it, she showed no time or love to me, perhaps she could never get to know me. What made her tick? I was well behaved and scared. I kept myself to myself; I rarely spoke or smiled and lost my confidence. I was truly on my own.

My sister Simone was the only family member I was drawn to. She understood certain sides of me, for she too had been brought up in a girl's home in Gravesend for five years. She was more aware of family life, she fought for her rights. She had class and was popular with her work friends, but never brought any home. She was ashamed of her home life and it hurt me. I was never to make friends and bring them back to a family home, it was just there to sleep and eat in. I couldn't wait to get out, but where to? Could I ever live alone in London, the city of lost souls?

I never spoke to adults and my mother never spoke to her fifteen year old son Paul. From her work friends, George's family and her Wimbledon Speedway friends I was to be hidden away, even from John Pearson upstairs, a kid my own age. We could never be friends, I would meet him on the stairs. I never spoke to him and he just gave me a shy smile. I longed for his friendship, his smile showed me that he wanted it too. I felt locked up inside, could I ever escape, could I ever be normal. I am sure John would like me. I needed his love and friendship. It was like this for two years, we would meet on the stairs. I must have been a sad case, quiet and lonely.

On Saturday I would travel on the underground all day, looking shy and smiling to anyone who noticed. How I longed for friends my own age. It was a cold and icy morning in early March 1961. I walked the half mile to east Putney underground station along familiar roads. Ahead of me were two fat ladies, I was quickly catching up to them. Behind me I heard footsteps. I turned around; it was the boy I had met many times on the stairs at Number 2, John Pearson.

'The railway lines are rusty and lead nowhere.'

"How are you Paul? Where are you off to?"

These were the first words John had ever spoken to me, and he knew my name was Paul. John was by my side. I looked at him, telling him I was going to spend the whole day travelling on the underground. These were my first words to him. How I wished he could travel with me, but...my mother.

"Paul, I have nothing to do, would you like company?"

Before I could answer the two fat ladies had fallen flat on their backs on the icy pavement. All I could see were four legs in the air, such a sight! I laughed and I laughed until I cried. John and I ran to the ladies, helping them up and steadying them. They kindly thanked us and said:

"No broken bones, thanks lads, such nice boys coming to our aid."

The ladies walked on.

"Well Paul, would you like my company on the underground?"

"John, do you mean it? Would you really like to come? Perhaps we could go to the flicks as well." I asked.

"Paul, I have seen you over the last two years and it's the first time I have seen you laugh, you always look so very sad. I could never understand that. My Mum and dad said; *Get to know him, we are quite sure he is not a misery but hurt inside. Be careful, get to know him.*"

John and I were inseparable, but it took two fat ladies to change my life and end two years of loneliness. At the time, I was listening to Perry Como's 'Magic Moments'. Funny how music can bring home the true meaning of friendship, like the friendship I had with John Pearson. The feeling never leaves me:

> *'To catch a falling star*
> *and put it in life's pocket,*
> *and never let it fade away...*
> *never.'*

A Slow Walk to Bury Park.

I had been living in a small room at the top of the old terrace house, number 109, for nearly two years. I liked living on my own, my thoughts to myself, my life to myself, my disappointments and sadness were part of my make up. I could work on my failings and strengths. Perhaps I was thinking too much; how was I going to change my ways? Maybe I was in need of a long walk to reflect, to work it out... What was it?

I longed to be like most of the people I met, smiling and outwardly happy, ready for the next laugh, meeting up for a drink at our local Marsh Farm pub, story telling, drinking pint after pint, being cheerful

109 Marsh Road, Leagrave.

around the warm atmosphere and regular faces, all speaking aloud. I looked around at the other people, young and old together. I had no right to be there. I walked slowly away from the familiar voices to the quiet streets of Leagrave on my own.

I was glad and relieved to walk along the Leagrave Road, past my small room at number 109, then quickly to Gardenia Avenue, which lay on the bus route towards the town of Luton, two miles away. I was glad to have the thinking time to clear my mind. Leaving the local shops in the distance, I passed the ABC Cinema showing the film 'Becket' on a sunny May afternoon. For me it was perfect cinema weather, but I was not in the mood to sit in a darkened room watching history in the making; too much was going on. I hardly noticed the people or their cries of laughter as they rushed by, quickly heading for Luton Football Club at Kenilworth Road; but the football season has ended? Or perhaps not.... reserves playing their heart out for the next season?

The hairdresser's shops seem to go on forever, growing dull and all around me; eighteen shillings for a blow wave with a cut, maybe some tinting? They all seemed to be hairstyles, all for eighteen shillings. Is that a lot for a hair-do? Or perhaps they go for a summer holiday chat and a place to rest their big fat arses. They are the nearest thing that women have to pubs, why don't they serve beer at the hairdressers? Perhaps they don't have a lavatory.

I go quickly on my way, happy to be on my own. I ask myself why I love music so much, which reminds me; I must go to Luton's newly built library and theatre to try out some classical music that I am constantly humming. I cannot get it out of my mind, what was his name? I can't remember... think Delrue. I have it! It's a little like my name, Delius, yes Delius, his music casts a spell over me, it puts me in moods of high heaven; all rolling hills and tall mountains. To think; Delius's music can do all that, how can it be? I can be in a summer garden one minute and by a river bank the next, peaceful, with my eyes looking towards strange and beautiful sunsets.

'I enjoy looking and yet not looking,
when the night draws near to the trees,
as though asleep.'

I walk much quicker to my goal, the High Street of Luton Town in full bloom. It's a fading town with many small shops, all white and black, all in need of repainting. I make towards the best shop in town, The Co-op, to pay my weekly account. I bought my tallboy for the grand sum of £12.00 including delivery, but I must pay it off in nine months. They're polite and friendly;

"How are you Paul? Nice to see you, how's the bookbinding going?"

I return their kind words with a shy smile of thanks. I go to the top floor for a cup of milky coffee and a slice of walnut and date cake. What an adventure, how happy I was, knowing nothing but the simple life, but I still couldn't get the tunes of Delius out of my head. I'm sure I heard the first cuckoo in spring early this morning, or was it a skylark? Such sad music, oh yes, it must have been a curlew, as he bids farewell to his mate and flies away, returning to feed his chicks; but one day he does not return home to his nest, he's no more in the air, long forgotten. I wish I could join him, I long to fly away, but I have to go to the library to pick up more of these sad stories on long playing records. Music all around me, music in the air, the open doors of heaven. I have been let in, why me? I am just a boy of nineteen, an apprentice bookbinder, travelling by train each day to the University College bindery. There they enjoy my love of classical music and often suggest music I might like instead of my friend Frederick Delius.

From the library I return to the Co-op, walk upstairs to the top floor and have a second milky coffee (without the cake). I sit in the corner, looking out of the window with a view of Luton shoppers, eager and unsmiling, with shopping on their minds. I notice the cake shops are doing good business, lots of Saturday teas perhaps. My mind drifts to my future plans, a comfortable feeling, my books bound at the Central School are doing well in competitions and I am well liked, even popular. I am more confident, but still afraid of myself, I could not let go of my past. I did not want to. I wanted to be back there in Enfield, to play in the meadow. I like the name 'Enfield' like I like the name 'meadow': meadow is the pleasure of a field of buttercups and of soft green grass I could lie in, taking my play clothes off, naked, with the sun warming me. I was on my own with the sun. I felt relieved to be on my own, my eyes wide and clearly open, looking up to the friendly yellow sun.

'Heaven sent me here.' I was back at St George's school, remembering how much I enjoyed gardening; it was warm, hard work. I was even given a small patch of garden overlooking the front of the school, my little patch was seen by all the pupils and teachers walking past. It was full of small coloured daisies, my very own little patch of colour. I bought a packet of 'Bee's Seeds' for four pence. I never thought for one minute that the seeds would show such loveliness. My small handkerchief garden was a personal success. I was congratulated by all and even managed to get a gold star for my efforts. My first gold star, a star of wonder perhaps? But I was not happy at St George's and was glad to start work at the King's Cross factory. I worked there for just a year and a half before the University College found me and started me as an apprentice hand bookbinder. There I would stay for ten years, returning once more to joyful happiness I had known at the boys' homes in Feltham and Enfield.

My thoughts flooded out as I sat sipping my milk coffee at the top of Luton Co-op, my thinking shop. It was all so easy and it felt good to be on my own, to be looking my best with the latest modern, showy clothes along with my regular, neat haircut. I gave a wholesome, good looking impression to the outside world and I noticed people looking at me for the first time. I wondered why; it never occurred that they might have fancied me and thought me good looking. I began to smile much more and would practice in the mirror. I had still not started shaving and I longed to be hairy like most others at my age, but other than that I was perfectly happy, as I had my independence and freedom. I had not seen my family for nearly two years. They were rarely in my thoughts and I wished I could say I missed them. My Putney days were behind me. I grew up in mind as well as in body. I was developing into a sensitive, thoughtful and interesting young man. I found a new inner confidence, I learnt to speak up, to be listened to and found I had a sense of humour, albeit a little different to the others. I was growing to love myself. I would buy new records each week, but always saved a little and the amount was slowly rising to over £100. How could I be so rich? I put away £2 each week at the post office in Euston Road every Friday dinner time.

I was rich and full of energy, raring to go to the musicals and jazz clubs of London with my new found friends. Lots of walking around the West End; I was busy taking it all in, not talking much, looking around, I was still very shy and indeed a little afraid of grownups. Could I ever be true to myself? I was yet to think about my future, or if I could ever make an impact. Friday was easily my favourite day. I got an extra hour in bed and would dress in my latest smart clothes. I tried not to overdo it, but I did wear a light fur coat for day classes. All the students at the Central loved and approved I think. I felt very beautiful, as if eyes were for the first time looking at this nineteen year old boy.

Beautiful hands.

Although I loved myself for the first time, and felt what it was like to be truly in love, still shyness was locked inside my head. I was not ready to be touched by another or to be kissed. I was very afraid of my inner self and could not let myself go.

As I returned to my little heaven 109, I remembered once again my mother's home in 2 Holmbush Road, Putney: A shared house with three other families all with children, except lovely old Mrs Bessant on the ground floor. I was unhappy and lonely there except for the boy John Pearson who lived upstairs in the top flat. John saved my life and we became firm friends, but I had to leave Putney to find myself. To live on my own. I valued privacy and had found my little room, all I wanted, living with my friends Reg and Jean, their little baby Sandra and Curley their cute black dog. It was a very cold April day two years ago that I waved unhappiness away at Putney. I left my usual £2.50 on the kitchen table for the last time and just walked out, taking an old worn suitcase that Mrs Bessant had kindly given me. I filled it with my clothes and a few books I had collected from the Upper Richmond Road bookshop. I was on my way. I turned around, hearing a familiar noise as she opened wide the kitchen window.

As I crossed the road carrying my old brown suitcase my mother shouted:

"You'll be back, you've got no friends!"

The pain of these few words still makes me sad just thinking. I hurried away, meeting John Pearson at East Putney station. He smiled and looked at my unhappy face.

"John, come with me to Luton and share my room, my friends won't mind."

"No Paul, I cannot leave my Mum and Dad, you see I am wanted and loved, I can't leave that, you understand. Give me your case and get a single ticket to your first real home in Luton with your friends. I will miss you. My family told me when we first met; *John get to know him, he's hurt inside, be his friend."*

As my train slowly left the platform John Waved me away, shedding clear white tears. I knew in my heart I that loved John and would miss him. John left the Putney house shortly after and went with his loving family to New Zealand. I never heard from John again, but I am sure we think of each other often, remembering the two fat ladies who fell on the slippery road as we walked together toward Putney underground station. I was always on my own when I spent the day on the underground, but my friend this time travelled with me. Before he left John wrote one letter to me, telling me that he will soon be off on new travels to New Zealand. I will always remember his last farewell to me, he ended his letter:

My love yours,
John P

It was the first time I had received a letter ending with love. I lived in my little room for nearly six years and often walked a slow walk to Bury Park to clear my mind, thinking of joy and happiness for the first time since I left the boys' home at St Joseph's Enfield, full of hope for the new future, my future, my life.

My Road to Damascus.

My first job was at the leather factory, at King's Cross, owned by Connolly Brothers. It was a late summer evening when I left Connolly's and, as always, headed for the corner café, where I had my usual order of baked beans on toast and a cold drink before heading up the Euston Road. Crossing the road at St Pancras Church, I made my way towards Russell Square until I reached Southampton Row and the Central School of Art and Crafts, in time for my first ever evening class at 6.30pm.

The Central School.

I was an idle walker, always humming, thinking quiet thoughts and inwardly grateful that I did not have to face the family back in Putney until ten, later in the evening. Suddenly, stopping short of the Central School of Art and Craft, I was struck by the realisation of just how poor and friendless I was. It was my 'Road to Damascus' moment.

I knew, from then on, that I was on my own and somehow had to make the best of things, I had to better myself. What to do? Who to trust? I knew I had to be strong in mind and will.

After sitting down on the steps for a few minutes, I took a deep breath and went in to the Art School. The notice on the second floor door read, 'Bookbinding'. I quietly entered the large, open room; everyone turned around, smiled and welcomed me to my first evening class.

It became easier and more familiar as time went on. At last, I had arrived and found the thing I had waited for, for so long. Something to put my trust in.

Over the Hill and Far Away, 1962-1967.

I lived with my friends Reg and Jean along with their little girl Sandra and scruffy dog Curley for five years at 109 Marsh Road, Leagrave, near Luton. It was a small three bedroomed terrace house, over a hundred years old, which had seen little modernisation over the years. It was a neat old fashioned house that needed attention, but then Reg was simply the best do-it-yourself man. Over the five years, along with my help, he made it into a palace; it was certainly the most beautiful little house I have ever lived in. I was given the back bedroom; a long, small room overlooking their scarf garden, with the railway line as my comfortable view. It was my first real home. I was happy

Paul's Haven

to furnish it myself with a neat single bed and bright coloured blankets, which matched the cheerful carpet and sunny curtains. All this bought from Heals in Tottenham court Road, London. I added a tallboy to put my 'latest fashion' clothes and beautifully polished shoes in, finishing off with my first ever wall book case and a small table for my Ferguson black and white television, which received two channels, BBC and ITV. Together with my record player my little room was complete. Reg kindly put in a small kitchen sink and housed my Baby Belling on an attractive

The Scarf Garden at 109.

cream painted table, all mod cons, and for the winter I bought a fan fire. I was set up and ready to go. I loved my independence; looking after myself for the first time and doing it well. I learnt to cook. My food cupboard was always filled with food that was good for you (via Sainsbury), two pounds per week my food bill. You could buy a lot in those days. My baked bean days were over.

Every two weeks I received an airmail letter from my sister Simone, she lived in America, working as a nanny for a lawyer family named Rice. They had three small children to look after. I saved her letters for years; they took me to another world, a world I could only read about in film magazines. She lived in a large modern house with the Rice's. They had a swimming pool and a very large garden which required a full time gardener. The house was only one of its type in Boston, Massachusetts. Each week she would go horse riding. She joined a theatre company called the Boston Players. Her interests were wide and her friendships many. She was given plenty of time to travel to New York, L.A., Mexico City, San Francisco, Salt Lake City, many places I had heard of in films, and, of course, she attended Hollywood night clubs and dinner parties, all in a mad heavenly rush. She would fly everywhere, was popular and beautiful, a real class act that I could never match, but never wanted to. Simone lived for excitement, going to Las Vegas for weekends with friends and living in posh hotels. The Rice's paid for everything; they treated her like one of the family. She got used to America, writing and telling me about Thanksgiving Day. She never cooked; they paid their own cook, of course.

So her life in the States was for her heavenly, but I loved my little bed sit at 109 Marsh Road, Leagrave, my own taste of freedom. I could come and go when I liked. It was my small homely world. I lived the excitement through Simone's letters and loved them, but I loved my world of improving my mind, listening to classical music, being an apprentice for University College, where I stayed for ten years. I bought my own small terraced house, my first home ever, I had made it. It was as though my whole world opened up. I walked around my small house, 136 Gardenia Avenue, Luton and hugged and kissed the bricks. My own home at last. I was twenty two and could not be chucked out. It was the security I longed for. I stayed there for five years, working on the house, making it like a palace, just like Reg and Jean had made 109 Marsh Road, Leagrave. They had help from their parents, I could only rely on myself. As my sister said years later:

"You did it yourself, you have no one to thank."

I received 'airmail' letters from Simone, her letters were always a great excitement to me and I enjoyed reading them in the laundrette. The launderette was just across the road from my little room in Leagrave, I lived there (until I bought my own house and married) from seventeen to twenty two. I went to the launderette every couple of weeks with my black Gladstone Bag full of dirty washing. Washing on Monday evening was a joy; watching the washing spinning in the machine, around and around. I was a familiar face, I would sit and watch my modern clothes as they

'This is what I hear all day; The trees singing my music, or I have sung theirs.'

were cleaned. They would come out smelling as fresh as the day they were bought from the Luton Boutique High Street Top Shop, 'for the up to date young man'.

I sat down on their surprisingly soft, comfy chairs, with my black bag between my legs and took out my airmail letter from my sister Simone and was taken into a different world. I slowly read the letter in which Simone told me that with friends, she had visited famous night clubs and had even been introduced to Bobby Darin! He was all the rage. The next week she met Connie Francis at the Rice's private party in Boston. She had spent the following days horse riding. She used to dance in the kitchen of No.2 Holmbush Road, using the hand towel hanging from the kitchen door as her partner. I was too shy to join in and could only watch her dancing to Dean Martin, or Del Shannon's 'Runaway'. She wore the old 45 record out, only then did she give it to me. I would put the record on the record player, which was battery powered. Often, as a treat I would buy new batteries. I loved that little record player; Uncle Loutche sold it to her for six pounds. I remember that the record that Simone loved above all was Bobby Darin's 'Mack the Knife'.

I spent most of my time, either in the kitchen or down stairs, alone or in that cold room, thinking always of the day I would have a room to myself, where I could listen to my own collection of records. With my first weeks wages I bought the E.P. 'Singing in the Rain'. I still have that record; I bought it from WH Smiths on Putney High Street, my favourite record shop. I would spend hours looking at Long Players, mostly jazz. I

'I am a little surprised by my dependence on music.' listened to Peggy Lee, and I also recall Dinah Washington singing 'September in the Rain'. I bought the hit single and also one from my favourite singer of all time, the wonderful Sarah Vaughan, but then I could change my mind the next week and be an Artie Shaw or Lena Horne fan. I loved her 'Stormy Weather' and Artie Shaw's 'Frenesi'. It was the first time I had listened intently to singers and their music; George Shearing took me by storm! My musical history lessons were on the first floor of W H Smiths with their five cubicles, where you could hear the records for the first time. It was in cubicle five that I first heard the strange jazzy sounds of Dakota Staton, singing off key, but magically 'My Funny Valentine'. I was to see most of my jazz heroes at places like 'The State' in Kilburn, 'The Palladium', 'The Gaumont' cinema in Hammersmith, Ronnie Scott's and so on. I lived on class acts for my three years at Putney, it was a way of hiding from my family.

It was during my apprentice years at University College Bindery and 109 Marsh Road, Leagrave that I found myself drawn to what was called 'classical music', the posh music. It came to me as naturally as breathing. I had a resentment of posh music and their long words. What was meant by a symphony or perhaps opera, a concerto, requiem and orchestra conductor? I was frightened and once again my lack of education held me back. I did not want those difficult, long musical phrases to get in the way. It was a new, unfamiliar world to me and it would not go away. I longed for more, it held me spellbound. It could not be understood and it awakened me unlike anything else. My first real musical experience was hearing a piece by Arnold Bax called 'Tintagel' in my little room (heaven). It was written or inspired by a vision of the sea, but I felt differently about it and was blown away by its melody and sound. How could it be done? How could music like this move me as never before? It had taken me over. I must listen to more of this classical music but I would have to keep it to myself, I could never reveal that I was falling in love with such posh music.

Each day was an excitement with sounds of lyricism and of yearning passion. Birdsong and the smell of the country is ever present, evoking bees, butterflies, the sound of water and above all nostalgia, melodies both yearning and tearful. Music could make a boy of eighteen feel all of that. I had to keep it to myself, but how could I keep it to myself? It was with me walking to Leagrave railway station each day, walking along Euston Road towards University College, humming my new sounds while I worked on my books all day. Walking up the road to get a pie for dinner, I was simply swamped with music, all classical. I had left the old world of Pop. I went to my local library in Luton and joined the record club, which is where I first found Frederick Delius. His lovely music has never left me. If I were forced to choose a piece of Delius it would be 'Prelude to Iremlin' (5 minutes long). Delius is the last great apostle of a time of romance, emotion and beauty in music. That's all I can say.

Of course, the music fired me to new heights; I loved the moving sound of 'Faure's Requiem' and the French school of Debussy; his 'Reverie' (a little piano piece), or Maurice Ravel's 'Opera les Enfant et les Sortileges' and Berlioz 'Les Nuits d'ete', the list could go on. I must return to the music that got me started, English music. The orchestral works of Edward Elgar come to mind, particularly his Symphony number Two, together with my favourite Violin Concerto. Elgar makes the music cry, a strange work unlike any other of his, a private work, a deeply thought out piece. Not forgetting of course, his 'Loves Greeting' known as 'Salut d'amour'. I cycled all over London Town with my friend Elgar at my side and was totally tuned into him, the countryside was never so beautiful as with Sir Edward. He made me English and alive and I fell in love with him. He was totally self taught, no Royal College of Music for him, moved always by his countryside of Worcester, his boyhood upbringing, to create a sound like no other. What is English music? Edward Elgar leads the way, followed by Vaughan Williams with 'Fantasia on a Theme' (originally by Thomas Tallis) which had deep roots in the English countryside. Have you ever heard of Ronald Binge? His 'Sailing By' captures my heart, a perfect gem. I also like George

Butterworth's 'Loveliest of Trees' with words by A.E. Houseman, so touching and poignant. But the most heart wrenching music ever is Peter Warlock's 'The Curlew' with words by W.B. Yeats, it is the mood of desolation; cry no more in the air.

An Eriskay Love Lilt

Traditional
Arr: Gilly Fordham

Vair me o, ro van o, vair me o, ro van ee, vair me o ru o ho. Sad am I with-out thee.

Out of the few songs I retain from the boys' home, one stands out. I first heard Sister Kathleen singing 'An Eriskay Love Lilt' in the mending room. I was waiting for her to sew a button on to my school shirt. I had to wait a further forty years till I heard it again. As a small child, it was kept inside my musical head for years before I discovered its strange name 'An Eriskay Love Lilt'. It makes me weep and I still feel the beauty inside. How can music move me in such a way, what gift has God given me? The sound of beauty has truly touched me, I have dreamed that I was in heaven. And now for the most difficult sound, the one I would leave behind, perhaps on my death bed when I am one hundred and nine. The last music on earth is Debussy's Prelude 'L'apres-midi d'un Faune' with Thomas Beecham conducting. I can now just fade away and never come back, who would want to?

Valerie Pearson.
By the Apprentice, 1964.

I was in my third year of apprenticeship with University College when I first met Valerie Pearson. She worked as a hand-sewer for the Bindery. She was in her mid thirties, attractive and intelligent. Unlike the other women who worked in the bindery, she took a particular interest in a boy of eighteen. She had been married, but that was when she was in her early twenties. It only lasted two years, they were not suited. She now lived in a beautiful flat in Parliament Hills Field, eight miles or so from the University College's bindery in London's Gower Street, and would get the underground to Euston Square. She was a little uncomfortable with men, but perhaps I was just a teenager and would listen to her every word. She was a wonderful adviser and we were able to talk freely to each other. It was said that Valerie took a fancy to me, but I was too innocent to understand her liking for me.

The Apprentice.

She had a boyfriend called Michael, but Michael was married and had two small children; boys of five and four. He loved his children. He was also a bookbinder, binding for Her Majesty's Stationary Office in Waterloo. Michael had started like me, and served an apprenticeship for H.M.S.O. bindery, completing it some years previously. Valerie fell head over heels for him and loved him dearly, but their relationship had to remain a secret, even from friends and family. Their relationship was difficult and strained, but their feelings for each other were strong and complete. Michael could never leave his two boys, they needed a father, even if he did not need a wife. Arguments often arose, it was the same old thing:

'Since I can never see your face, And never shake you by the hand, I send my soul through time and space, To greet you. You will understand.'

"Michael, you have to choose between me and the boys."

"But I can't. How can I let you go Valerie?" He said tenderly, with tears in his eyes;

"You mean the world to me."

Their time together was sometimes as near to heaven as it was to hell.

103

"I wish we had never met in the Pub two years ago, Christmas time. You were sitting alone, looking into your drink, playing with your turkey sandwiches. You looked sad and far away. I left my friends and sat in the corner table opposite you. You looked up and caught me looking at your hazel eyes, they were full of sad regrets and longing. I was afraid. You came over to take the empty chair next to me and we never stopped looking at each other and talking. We fell for each other at that moment, over the turkey sandwiches!

"Your friends left us in peace, they sensed our being together and knew I was unhappily married. I often talked about it to my workmates. We had been married for nearly ten years. We were just not suited and thought that children would pull us together. I loved my boys, but right from the start I worried that getting married was a mistake. She loved me, but I never felt it. I always held back. Night time was lonely and I cheated on her. Then you, Valerie, came along, ten years too late. You were all that was missing from my sad, unhappy life. You lifted me up, I loved being with you. Talking and wishing for some kind of miracle. Your eyes held me spell bound, you looked at me and somehow made me complete.

"I longed always to be with you, but we had to live in secret. The pain of returning home to my married life with food on the table and my boys, excited at seeing me, talking and playing with me. They were football mad, the Hammers being their team. Every two weeks I would take them to Upton Park, the treat they looked forward to more than anything. I loved that excitement, mine for you and theirs for their football team. Oh, the pain of returning home to pretend I loved my wife, it was beginning to be like a prison sentence. I was behind bars, it was the boys that held me together."

Michael was mad keen on cars and shared his interest with the boys. His wife was only interested in Michael, her life was utter devotion to Michael, she was a proud, good, honest wife, to everyone around she and Michael were the perfect couple. Their life was a sham, he knew it and hated himself for such a deception. When he left her for work he gently kissed her goodbye and returned in the early evening to be kissed on his lips. The boys rushed to be picked up and hugged and kissed, it was an honest moment, the boys were his life. How he held them tight and would only let go when his wife shouted "Tea is on the table." He hated bedtime the most, her comely body revolted him, her nakedness sickened him. He undressed quickly and got into the bed, covering himself up and turning off the lights at the same time. Reading and talking, until sleep called... It called slowly, every night was very long.

"How do Michael and you live like that?" What pain.

On our first meeting at the Pub, Valerie opened her heart to me:

"Paul, you are like a young Michael, I can easily talk to you, you say nothing, just listen. But believe me, as we got use to each other Michael changed, we relaxed and I was free. I lived for our meetings and our few weekends together. He lit up and could talk eagerly about so many subjects. Michael, like me was a great reader. Paul, do you read?"

"Sorry, I was not brought up on books."

I read very little at the boys' home, none of the kids did. I left the boys' home at fifteen and could hardly read or write. I could not even fill in forms, my education was of sports and crafts. I was always good with my hands and basketry and painting of course. I loved painting people and trees. My paintings were always of sad boys crying, for they had no where to live and they were lonely and poor. I could paint and draw the boys from St Vincent's and St Joseph's. Valerie, I was in a boys' home for 15 years, there was little learning, but I was quite good at games and when I was on my own I loved to dance, but I was afraid in case I was caught or seen by any of the other boys, I don't know why. I would dance with the furniture, spinning chairs around, lifting the chairs lightly onto the wooden tables. I jumped up onto the tables, lightly sat on the chairs and balanced my slim body, turning around and around until I held onto the chair, and carefully jumped back onto the worn front room carpet. I would land with hardly a sound, except that of the Billy Cotton Band on the wireless. I always listened out for other boys, perhaps I was afraid they would catch me and called me a sissy.

At the boys' home it was all sport and muscle, rarely was any gentleness shown, but the Sisters liked me for I was a good altar boy and practiced kneeling and genuflection. I was a beautiful altar boy Valerie, my movements were like dancing, I practiced being holy and saintly. I looked the sisters straight in the eye, it was the only time I was at home. I was comfortable wearing my black and white cassock, and walking lightly I gave the Priest the altar wine and water, ringing the bells and answering in latin verse. I looked good, I know I felt honest and beautiful, I believe I was nearer to God then than at any other time of my life. I felt that when I left the home, I should become a Priest or perhaps the Pope, for I truly believed in all things Christian and good. It was the only time I fell in love, it was special to be God's altar boy, to serve him, to smile and be safe as I walked along the polished parquet floor. Living my altar boy act, I would put my hands together as though in prayer. I was truly touched by Jesus' love.

St Joseph's Chapel.

The Sisters with their heads bowed and hiding between their hands, opened their fingers so as to look at me. That slow walk finishing Mass was my act of Glory to God on high. The small church was deathly silent, other than my quiet footsteps. I was thinking of tomorrow's service; must ring the bell a little lighter. I was in heaven. But Valerie that was three years ago, I remember as though it were yesterday, but I have changed. My thoughts are not so simple, I don't even go to church and I don't feel bad about it. I hate grown ups and never want to be a grown up, they lie and bully you with harsh words. I am not looked after Valerie, my family were a real disappointment. I went to live with them after the boys' home in Enfield, with my mother and her family. I was not wanted and I was unhappy, but all ends well as I now live alone, sharing a house with friends just outside Luton. I am happy there, for the first time. Come and visit me I am sure my friends would put you up, they are very kind.

Valerie never did visit. We always had our sandwiches in the park during our work break, she from hand sewing, me from my apprenticeship. Our talks were of intimacies, she was so very curious about my childhood, my lost family of Putney and my other interests. She filled me with hope, for the first time in my life I felt valued and safe in her company. The warmth of her voice, her sunny smile, her sense of humour, of fun. She was some kind of woman. She wore little makeup and always dressed simply and elegantly. She was the first woman I fell for, not out of anything other than just to be valued. I thought highly of Valerie Pearson, she always made my day. She was at the college bindery for just seven months. For weeks she had looked forward to going to the Motor Show at Earls Court, Olympia with Michael all to herself. It meant a lot to me to see her so happy. I simply wished her an enjoyable weekend and looked forward on Monday to hearing all about the Motor Show, eating our cheese sandwiches in our usual Bedford Square Park, just minutes from University College Bindery.

But Valerie did not turn up for work as usual, which was not like her. She was never late for work, it worried me. John Vivian answered the bindery telephone, late morning. The caretaker of her building had decided to break open her Flat door, which was on the second floor, number 7. He had telephoned John Vivian to say that Valerie was dead. She had gassed herself. She'd let her cat out and laid in front of the gas fire. The police were in her flat and the ambulance men had just recovered her body. John Vivian, the Bindery Supervisor took me to one side and explained as best as possible that Valerie had committed suicide. It seemed she left a note for her friend Michael. He was going to leave her and return to his family, but she says to tell the young friend, the apprentice, please miss me and forget me.

I cried remembering her loss. It was the first time death was so final.

I loved Valerie.

Thinking Like All The Rest.

When I was 15 years and did not understand the world,
My hopes hardly showing themselves,
I cried more easily and laughed more openly,
There was no bitterness, I was hardly aware of myself,
No one had told me or made me
What I was to become.

I was new and alive,
Life had not made its troubles upon me.
I cared only about myself
For I was not lost by the complications of older beings,
I was set and ready to go,
Alas I am twenty five years on, and hold my head in shame.

Thinking like all the rest.

Peter's Palace.

It seems such a long time ago that I bought my first little house near Biscot Parish Church, in Leagrave, Bedfordshire. It was a neat terraced house with a nice open garden running down to the Primary School playing fields. The children would politely shout "Thanks Mister!" as I regularly returned their light plastic football.

My small black dog loved the children; I had recently bought him from the dogs' home in Dunstable, with his sad face and bright brown eyes. He was not a good guard dog at all. He seemed to smile whilst wagging his tail at all callers and rarely barking, but he was perfect and friendly. After work I would take him for a long walk up the road on a slight hill, past the school and on to the park. Then I'd return to number 136 Gardenia Avenue, my house, where I would change into my old working clothes; jeans, a worn shirt and comfortable old, soft shoes, ready to transform the shabby building I had bought six months earlier.

The first job was to make sure my front door looked friendly and smart. I painted it my favourite colour, bright green, and treated it to a brass handle and bell. It was the happiest looking door in the whole of Gardenia Avenue, bright and shiny.

Next, I decided that the house was dark and gloomy so I decided to let in the light with glazed interior doors, which brightened every corner. It became my dream house, my first real home and I spent many hours turning it into a small palace. After a comforting, cheap bite to eat I would put my latest Mahler Symphony on the record player, never tiring of the music that helped me to think while I was busy decorating. I painted and papered my little two up-two down house with its 'cowboy bath' and front passageway, all in the company of my nameless black dog who rarely barked.

With my work as a bookbinder at University College in London and improving my little house, I had lots to look forward to. Whilst I listened to Mahler I thought about my life. Whether it would have been different if I had been brought up by a mother and father, especially a father. What would it have been like to have had a man in my life to look up to? What would he have been like? Would he have had a room of his own, growing up? Would

Peter's Palace.

he have enjoyed listening to Mahler or playing the trumpet or piano? Perhaps he painted pictures or was clever with his hands? I just wanted to have an image of such a man, to have touched his face and been held by him. All these questions raced round in my head. Were his own parents interested in him? Was I like him? Did he have a kind face? Was he fair and slight like me, with eyes the same coloured blue as mine? I was sure he would be good at wallpapering and decorating and would help me out. Did he have a feeling for those who could not help themselves and would he have looked out for the smaller boys bullied by bigger ones?

At this moment I would think of the reality of my own life, of a father too cowardly to protect others and one who had never tried to look for his boy growing up in a children's home, or imagined what it would be like to be without a father.

The older I grew the more important the idea of a father's presence meant to me and as the years went by I thought of nothing else. I wondered if he would ever come knocking at my newly painted, bright green front door and in my mind I would step down from my ladders to answer the shiny brass doorbell; but no-one was ever there.

Sometimes for hours, I'd feel sad and unwanted but I had a tendency to overcome all the longing and think of happier times with my three childhood friends from St Vincent's Boys' Home, in Feltham. Jeremy, Terance, Lawrence and I were inseparable, always working hard and playing together in our tree house, fighting and rolling about in the school playing fields where nobody could find us. We took turns seeing who could pee the furthest, laughing and comfortable with ourselves. When we were eleven years old and I was taken to the other boys' home in Enfield, my three friends went off to live with their parents. I cried as I waved them goodbye, missing them terribly, as I still do. Sunny, bright-eyed, perfect friends. It could never last.

Then I'd think of my father. When I was just thirteen years old I was told that my father had been in the RAF, dying in the Far East in late 1945 (the story often changed). I did not break down, I couldn't take in the reality that I had never met or seen my father but I knew I would have loved to hear his voice, the voice calling me "Son" or saying, "Boy, it's time for bed!"

"Oh" you might say, "What does it matter?" But readers, it really matters to me. Perhaps I would have been a fuller person, not dwelling on my past so much. It is not good for me but it haunts me. I need to know the clues to my character and life, to feel what it would have been like to have had a 'normal' life with parents, brothers and sisters, receiving all the Christmas and Birthday cards that I never did as a child.

One evening, as my thoughts ran this way, the doorbell rang. Or did it? I waited paste brush in hand, about to continue when the bell rang for a second time and unusually, my black dog barked. I hurried to the front door and there on the front step stood a boy of about nine years of age, anxiously looking up at me.

"Please, Mister, can I take your dog for a walk? I promise to be very careful with him."

The boy was neat and tidy, in grey shorts and jumper with an overcoat on top. He looked cold and apprehensive as he asked for the second time if he could take the dog to the park, all the time looking me straight in the eyes, (very brave of him, I thought).

"Tell me what your name is, where do you live and how did you know I had a dog?"

He hesitated and then answered:

"My name is Peter and I live with my mum and younger brother who has the same name as you, Paul. We live down the road in a flat on the second floor and my mum sees you through the kitchen window walking past. Our flat is too small to have pets but I've always wanted a dog of my own and one day I will, I tell mum."

"Come in out of the cold but mind the paint and paper." I said. "You can take my dog to the park but you must be careful of the busy roads. I'd like you to give my dog a name, too."

"Can I call you Paul, like my young brother?" he asked.

"Of course you can, and I'm sorry if I frightened you when I answered the door. Now, here is the lead and I feel sure that my dog is in good hands. Take as long as you like."

As I passed him the lead, Peter's eyes were on me and he smiled widely as he thanked me.

"My mum told me that you had a kind face, and she was right, you are nice." he beamed as he took my black dog on his first walk.

The following Saturday he returned and I asked him if he had thought of a name for my dog.

"Yes, but last night my brother Paul was very sick and my mum had to call the doctor from the public telephone box round the corner. Paul and I share a small bedroom and I was really worried, but after the doctor gave him the yellow pills he slept the rest of the night. Mum was very worried all night long, holding his hand until he fell asleep."

I told Peter I was truly sorry to hear about Paul and told him to promise to tell his mother that she could always use my telephone, night or day.

"Peter, you don't have to tell me, but do you have a father?" I asked quietly.

"Yes, I have a dad but he left us when Paul was still a baby and we have not seen or heard from him since. I love my mum but she cries a lot, thinking about him."

Peter obviously missed his dad and longed to have him home. Quite out of the blue he held my hands tightly and embraced me, wiping his eyes on my shirt-sleeves and resting in my arms. He needed me, and I knew that I would have to be the father to him that I would one day be to my own son. He was affectionate and brave and I promised to be the friend and father that he so needed.

"Now you have two friends" I said, "Me and our little black dog. Now, what is his name?"

"I would like to call him Midnight."

"I like that name very much indeed but how did you come up with it?"

"I couldn't sleep last night, worrying about Paul. It was midnight before I closed my eyes and it was midnight on my mind when I woke to find my brother was well. I thought that would make a lovely name for your dog."

"Let's call it our dog Peter, and you can take him out anytime."

Peter called daily to have tea with me and we became friends. He did well at school and worked hard at home; shopping, keeping the house clean and cooking, while his mother worked at the Skefko Ball-Bearing factory. He was a great help to me too; mixing sand and cement and holding doors while I put in the new hinges and fittings, even helping when I fitted my new kitchen.

All this he did to please me, always greeting me with a hug, entirely happy and relaxed. When I took him to Luton, for a change, we went to the Wimpey Bar in the High Street, which he loved. I really wanted him to enjoy his childhood, coming and going as he pleased, and I was thrilled that he liked the cinema. Sometimes his younger brother would come with him after asking their mother first. I was touched by the way they held each other's hands. We went on the bus to Luton town and I couldn't help wishing they were less well-behaved, less caring and insistent on paying their own way.

"Peter," I would say, "I wish you would give me the pleasure of allowing me to spoil and treat you sometime."

One special day I was given a birthday present. It was a birthday cake Peter's mum had made and I was thrilled. Life that year was a rare pleasure. He and his brother brought cheerfulness and excitement to 136 Gardenia Avenue, telling me how much happier their mother was, and of their successes at school and football.

One evening, Peter was playing with Midnight and I was giving the garden a good turnover with the spade. I must have had that haunted look on my face because Peter came over to my side at once.

"Peter, something is on my mind. I can understand your pain at missing your father, because I long for a father too... My father was killed when I was just two years old. I never met him and he never married my mother, so I was looked after in a boys' home. Do you know what that is?"

"Yes." he nodded "How long were you living in the boys' home?"

"Until I was fifteen" I said. "I always felt I would have loved a father, that's all Peter, and I wanted to tell you because I love you as if you were my real son. Do you think your mum would mind if I took you to London, for a holiday? We could go by train from Leagrave."

"I'm sure mum would be thrilled, because I've never been

to London."

True to his word, Peter asked his mum and she agreed, knowing that Mr Delrue would take care of her son. He promised that he would bring back a gift for her and his brother Paul. London was a thank you treat, after all his hard work helping me with my house. For a ten year old he could work really hard and of course, his younger brother promised to look after Midnight. So we were on our way.

I suggested all the things he might like to do; walking round Covent Garden Market, Piccadilly Circus and Leicester Square. He took it all in. We even went to the flicks to see 'King Arthur' and he loved it. Peter's biggest treat was travelling on the Underground. I let him be as free as a bird, doing whatever he wanted. We ate in a Soho restaurant and our London trip was just perfect. I played my greatest role: I became a father to Peter.

Back in Leagrave, Peter spent the summer with me. I gave him the spare house keys. He came and went as he pleased, sometimes staying over in my spare bedroom with Midnight for company. I trusted him completely. He helped out in the garden, and if that summer the garden looked colourful, neat and attractive, most of the work was down to young Peter. He loved gardening and cutting the small lawn. Each day he called in with Paul to take Midnight out to play; they were very close to each other.

It was very sudden when Peter called round earlier than usual, one Friday evening. He looked frightened and sad. His father had returned home and was arranging for them all to leave Leagrave, moving to work and live in Ireland, his homeland.

He promised he was going to be the father Peter had always hoped for (how lucky for him, to have such a son). Peter looked lost and scared, reminding me of our first meeting outside my newly painted bright green door, the previous September. It suddenly seemed a long time ago. Peter said they were to set off early the next morning and that his father had told him to thank Mr Delrue. He then handed me a letter from his mum that I put away in my back pocket.

"Peter, I hope very much that your life in Ireland will be

a happy one, I truly mean it. I will miss your visits and hearing all about your family. You and Paul deserve to be happy, as a complete family."

I held my head downwards because I didn't want Peter to see that I was crying. He walked away to my green front door and rang the bell one final time, Midnight jumped up excitedly. Peter turned around, looking at me and then ran towards me, holding me tightly in his small arms and kissing me. I had never felt so loved and I have lived on Peter's love, ever since.

He walked away from my home at 136 Gardenia Avenue for the very last time. The evening was all lit up, glowing in the bright, warm sunshine. I hadn't the heart to wave goodbye but Peter turned slightly with a wave of a kiss, his final goodbye.

I was never to see Peter again, always wondering if he would remember me, the loving father-figure, without a father.

Before I went to my sad sleep, I remembered Peter's mother's letter, which I had folded and put in the back pocket of my jeans. It was crumpled and I had to flatten it out to read. It said this:

"Thank you, Paul, for everything you have done and given to my lovely son, Peter. He told me all about you and your early days at the boys' home without a family and how your father was killed in the war. But, dear Paul, you have a great capacity for a father's love; how do you learn that? My Peter will never forget you, I promise. My love, Peter's mum, Gloria."

This happened such a long time ago. I did finish the work on my terraced house, but it never felt the same. I named my little house with the bright green front door and smart brass bell 'Peter's Palace'.

Yes, I did hear from Peter, who wrote often with good letters. He is married, with a son, Paul, named after me. He lives in Brighton, listening to Mahler in the evenings as he works away happily on his small terraced house, his family home.

On fine summer evenings I shall walk along paths,

Pricked by wheat stalks, trampling the fine grass,

Dreaming and feeling the coolness on my feet,

I shall let the wind rush through my hair,

I shall not speak, I shall not think,

But endless love will rise up in my soul,

And I shall go far, far way like a gypsy,

Through the countryside

Happy as with boys.

For Peter

147 Dane Road,

Coventry.

CV2 4JU

16th April 1977

Dear Paul Delrue,

It was a great shock to receive your letter. I am still a bit mixed up about what happened all those years ago. But nevertheless I am the person you are seeking, as all the facts ring true. I remember your mother well and I know we were deeply involved but we parted and I went away, eventually ending up in the Far East for two years.

In spite of your early setback I see you are in your own business, I hope you are doing well. I am in the engineering trade and have been all my life. It is only natural you should be curious about the past. I shall try and get to see you, my wife and I have talked it over and she agrees I should try and make the trip next month all being well.

Yours Sincerely,

J.S. Payne

Remember Always, you have a Son.

I first met my father in 1977. He came always with his wife Bea. They visited me and my growing family three times. I remember very little about their first visit. He, with his wife by his side, spoke vaguely, the words I hardly remember. It was a long time ago and many questions were left unanswered. Our conversations always seemed trivial. How was the trip from their home in Coventry to ours in Caerwys, in North Wales. How long did it take, what was the traffic like? It went on like this throughout their visits. Yes, they had just returned from Scotland, where they had spent two weeks on their summer holiday.

He asked me very little about my early life. He had not been aware of my existence, for he had left Louise, my mother, knowing nothing of her pregnancy. He went to the Far East with the Army and wrote to my mother often. When my mother told him she was 'expecting', he never answered the letters again. Just waved goodbye and let her get on with it. I was to do without a father. I believed my mother's explanation. She had nothing to lose after all those years.

"Paul, I thought he was dead, that's what Jack's family had told me."

She believed it, why not? She even went to Jack's house in Coventry just after the war, the house was empty. She never looked for him ever again. But she did leave me with a major clue. Jack was always on about his posh middle name 'Spencer', he liked it. It was given to him by his father, a family name. If all was different I would be answering to Spencer instead of Paul.

At Jack's last visit I suggested we went for a drink in our local, 'The Piccadilly', where we could speak more freely away from his wife. It worked, but it left me disappointed. Was I like him? I shall never know. Was he interested in music, did he like making things with his hands, was he keen on painting, the arts, and reading, just like me? Jack told me he had two children.

Brenda, the first born in 1948 and Spencer, the boy. He seemed shy when telling me about them. I think that Bea had told him to say very little. We must keep 'our little secret' from our family, back home in Coventry.

As we sat in the quiet pub, all my questions flooded out, I had so much to say:

"Jack, what do you do for a hobby? Do you love getting dirty? Are you more often than not under that old veteran car? Jack, remember when you go to wash your hands ready for tea that you have a son. Jack, you tell me you always take your son Spencer and meet up with your work friends at Coventry City football matches. Jack, when Coventry score the winning goal and you raise your hands excitedly in the air, remember that you have a son. When you have a posh dinner to celebrate your wedding anniversary and you cut the icing on the cake, remember that you have a son. Jack, when you go to bed in silence, having kissed your wife goodnight, remember always Jack, you have a son".

I noticed a tear falling into his beer. I never saw or spoke to him again.

•Jack Spencer Payne Born Brighton 2 June 1924.

•Royal Navy, Joined 1943?

•Royal Navy, Discharged 4 December 1946.

•Married to Beatrice Maude Turner, 31 March 1947.

127 Dane Road,

Coventry,

CV2 4JU

24th May 1978

Dear Paul,

I hope this letter finds you all in good health. All the poor weather we have had recently does not help, as for ourselves Bea has been the main sufferer with a bad attack of the flu. Then her mother died a fortnight ago and she is just getting over it.

As regards you invitation I am afraid I have got to disappoint you. Having thought it over for a long time I do not intend to visit again. I have answered all your questions and satisfied your curiosity. So I have done all I planned to do. You expected more I know, that is life.

Things are not too good here in the engineering, but it's a general phase at the moment. Trust your work is picking up and you are making progress. Well Paul not a very cheerful letter but I hope you understand.

Yours,

Jack

Never as you. *A poem by Louise Wraffle.*

TAKE THE WORD OF MAN

(which is greater than the
word of God, in it's pain
and self-conception)

AND CURVE ROUND IT,
MORE INTRICATE THAN SUNSET,
AND MORE GENTLE.

BLEED A LITTLE WITH THE WRITER,
CARRESS WITH THEM, AND WEEP.

FOR ONLY A FEW WILL UNDERSTAND
AND THEY, NEVER AS YOU.

Written for Paul, Ruthin 1981

Binding to my Feelings.
(A speech to the Arts Workers Guild, London 2010.)

I left my comfortable, large home in Enfield, North London to become an apprentice Bookbinder for University College. It was on my day-release at the Central School of Art and Craft, not far from here in Queen Square, that I discovered a different kind of bookbinding. It held me spellbound, that you could express yourself and put on the covers almost anything, if you had the skill!

Could I ever have the skills? Could I work morning noon and night to achieve such heights? I had no idea, first of all I had never been art trained. Could I ever have the discipline, the commitment, but above all I knew I would have to fight my nature, to improve myself, to express myself. I had always had a colourful imagination and was quite good at drawing and working with my hands, but that was at school in Enfield. Now I had to be on show alongside the other apprentices. Most of the kids came from Trade Binderies and were more advanced than me. They seemed full of themselves and cocky, relaxed and good at table tennis.

I was just fifteen, shy and rather frightened of the much bigger and older boys, but that was only in my head. Very soon we were to become firm friends and I found I could beat them at table-tennis and billiards, but above all bookbinding came easily to me. It made me popular as I was asked by the older apprentices to help with their headbands, finishing, hand-titling, paring leather and even simple designs for their books.

It was at evening classes that I noticed the sweet little old ladies who were a little afraid of George Frewin, Fred Wood and Les Knight, the teachers. The ladies asked me to help them with their worn, tatty volumes. They would show their appreciation by bringing along sweet-meats: I was lean in those days, ladies and gentlemen! But that was fifty years ago, a lifetime ago. I was to stay at University College Bindery for ten years before going it alone, to see if I could earn a living, bring up my family and pay my mortgage. I think I succeeded: I now live and work in Wales. I live in a small country town called Ruthin, all at peace and rather beautiful. Often I would look back to my University College days in London town, thinking how lucky I am to have the hills of Wales for friends and noticing the season's changes.

I wonder what sort of a binder I have become? Let me put it like this; ever since I bound my first design binding at fifteen, in 1959 (which had a huge impact on me), I have noticed that bookbinders have their own style, they use unusual materials, many work in abstraction, some keep up the traditional skills of gold-tooling, much sought after by collectors. Some bind to technique, maybe pattern work, onlays and inlays, mostly modern. Where do I fit in? For I bind to my feelings; I can't help it. I cannot design to colour by numbers, which was what I was brought up with in the early days at the Central School and University College. I cannot get excited over pretty patterns, perhaps wallpaper patterns would do? Abstract binding comes too easily to me, it feels like cheating and you can make anything fit the binding; but colour and feeling is what I long for.

I hoped to bind that way, but now, perhaps I would have to leave the traditionalists behind, marvel at their skills but endeavour to go my own way, 'My Way', as Paul Anka would say, or was it Frank Sinatra?

My first Delrue (My Way) binding was 'Head Hunters of Papua New Guinea' in 1964. This was bound in Khaki-colour, Oasis Morocco, with black onlays and details made of ladies' white kid evening gloves, with its delicacy of fine silhouette face expressed in black leather onlays. It took me a year of day-release classes at the Central school, in London. I bound it when I was nineteen and still think, after all these years, it was the best effort I could manage. I knew it was a special binding and different to that of the other students. I was binding to my feelings, for the first time, and not an inch of gold passed my lips, other than the title. I was freed from the old fashioned decoration; the tradition of years, the comfortable years.

I have brought my first serious binding along to show you, all cut out using a paring knife and many months of skill. I dared to depict a face in black leather onlays and, as the printing world said:

"Delrue has used the black onlays in silhouette!"

Anyway, it got me noticed. I was, indeed, lucky unlike the Trade Binders I met at the Central School. University College allowed me to become a fine craftsman and not to seek recompense. I was a quick learner and bookbinding came easier to me than most of my fellow apprentices.

My next design binding that got me noticed, was my first ever commission, from Professor Richard Freeman, Professor of Zoology at University College. It won me a prize at the 1966 Harrison Exhibition held, in those days, at the National Book League, just off Green Park.

'English Insects'

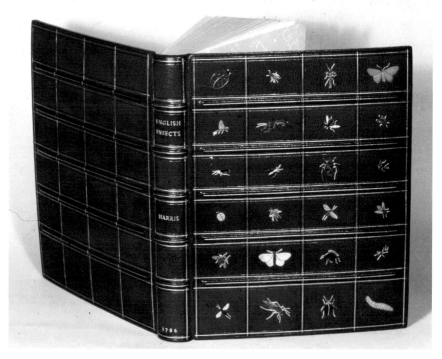

In early 1967 I had been asked by Howard M. Nixon, the Deputy Keeper of the British Museum, to hold myself in readiness to go to Florence because the River Arno had overflowed its banks and vast amounts of water had swept through the streets in currents as rapid as forty miles an hour. It devastated libraries, churches

and many shops; it was the worst disaster in the history of the city of Florence.

The College put me forward to join other British bookbinders. I was able to do my bit in the book baths, washing early books and worked with the Italian students of my own age. Most of the British binders were old pro's and had been binding for years at the British Library. I felt out of place with so many experienced binders. Who was I but an apprentice for University College, winning a few prizes, and did I deserve to be amongst the great and the good? They were binders with years of experience and a wealth of knowledge of paper repairs, historians and craftsmen of long standing. My memory was of serious British bookbinders talking over a cup of tea about what they would be doing the next day...work, work, work.

But what could I do? I had never been abroad but the College wanted me to go and I could not let them down: I had been spoken of as, 'The Boy Wonder Bookbinder' and so I nervously said yes. I was flying off to Italia, this boy from St Vincent's Boys' Home. The beauty of Florence overwhelmed me and my favourite meeting place was the Ponte Vecchio (The Old Bridge) which spanned the Arno. It is a picturesque construction lined with shops on both sides (nearly all gold and silversmiths working away) and there is even a bust of Benvenuto Cellini on

Ponte Vecchio.

it. I spent two months there. It is true that all Florentines will remember that Friday of November 4th as the date my beloved bridge, the Ponte Vecchio was submerged and swallowed up by the raging waters.

I fell in love with Florence, but back home I returned to dull grey London, to finish my apprenticeship at University

Italian students washing the books (Paul second from the back).

College and complete my time. I continued to bind; masterpieces perhaps for the annual competition. It always thrilled me when I came across bindings, beautiful bindings and wondered how it was done? Puckering caught my attention, inlays beautifully done, interesting gold tooling, I'd never seen anything like it. They certainly were not binding that way at the college or day classes. They kept very much to the old traditions. What way should I go? Who could guide me and help? I was losing my way, perhaps.

130

The English boy abroad.

Help did come when I was left alone to sort out my binding pictures; that's how I saw my bindings, pictures to fit the book. So I came up with my answer in 1966 for the 'Harrison Binding' of 'English Insects', to combine the old with the new. Gold decoration with insects made of small pieces of coloured leather, vellum, parchment, snake and lizard got me just the effect I had in mind and my teachers just left me alone to work it out.

The bookbinding judges must have liked it. It did well at The National Book League and did the college proud, but still I felt it was not the answer; that came years later. I was still binding by numbers, trying puckering and gold decoration, with which I never felt comfortable. How could I create what was in my head? What did I like or, easier, what didn't appeal?

Throughout my many years of bookbinding I had always used the leftover scraps of leather to make leather pictures. I began to make leather pictures with greater ease and so I decided to transpose my pictures onto my bindings, after all I had been told by a number of well known binders that my design bindings looked like pretty pictures. I took it to heart. It was their criticism of me and my work, but I carried on nevertheless. Why not use the book as my canvas? I was comfortable, at last. The Delrue way from leather pictures to book covers worked an outcome I had never seen before... It created an atmosphere. Starting with the endpapers, edge colouring, mixing coloured leather together,

Underneath the arches.

The River Arno.

feeling my way. As soon as the 'pretty picture' developed I could change it, like a painting. I could ply leather on leather and sand away the unwanted; I could mount an impression, not the clear cut images I had grown up with. A feel for the book's contents, the printed page, from the outset in my mind's eye I chose colours that most bookbinders dared not use. I could build houses, country views, images all around me, yellow trees, elephants, flowers. I could create sadness, loss, an imprisoned soul. It all began with a binding I carried out using Connolly Brother's cow hide from the leather factory I first worked in, at King's Cross as a boy of fifteen. I have a sneaking feeling, all along, that I have always bound to my feelings, except that it is even stronger than I imagined.

I wish I could plan it on paper or on a computer, but I was never good at Tech. drawing, although I could paint a little. I've always seen the book as alive and in colour. I can't help it.

Master and Apprentice - A Time Recalled.
John Charles Vivian.

DAY 1: _June 1, Llandudno; a glorious sunny day._

I became an apprentice at University College, London in 1961 having just turned 16. I knew right from the start what I had let myself in for. I'd always been good with my hands, so bookbinding was a comfort and a joy. To be frank, it was just perfect. My presentation is not of facts and figures. It is my thoughts and recollections of my first ten years as a bookbinder and of the characters who set me on my way.

Let me introduce you to the team. The person in charge, the bindery supervisor, without an OBE, Mr John Charles Vivian.

Then, Mr Denham, the great forwarder and wonderful fun. I also had the excitement of the women sewers. Funny really, they were content to sew all day long. They always complained that the backs of their legs were cold. The chief sewer was Mrs Hamilton. She was an elderly lady, classy but overbearing. She travelled up from Bromley - hardly anything to sniff about. The next in line was the delectable Valerie Maiden, a slender gal who was in awe of 'Lady' Hamilton.

We had two roses; Rose Willett, of a kind and worrying nature, (she always remembered the boy's birthday) and Rose 'the nose' Hutton, a real cockney Londoner. Behind her back we called her hooky. I hope she is not in the audience. She was great fun. And finally the boy; that was me!

The women took turns in making the tea and were very happy to do so. Once I went round to the women's section and told Mrs Hamilton that the kettle had boiled. I thought I was doing her a good turn. She ignored me and carried on overcasting. I said a little louder:

"Mrs Hamilton, the kettle has just boiled. Would you like to make the tea now?"

She didn't look up. Just chose to ignore me. The helpless, useless boy. I turned to young Valerie and told her that the kettle had just boiled. Valerie gave me a nervous smile. Mrs Hamilton put down her sewing needle and looked up at me.

"How can I help you?" she said.

"The kettle has just boiled, would you like to make the tea?" I asked.

She replied with half a smile that it was the water boiling and not the kettle. I never went round there again; I left the tea making duties in their court and good luck to them. I can't understand it really. She only came from Bromley. A wonderful

'An artist must do this,
He must select and transmit material given,
be true in his account,
and line the canvas
with his words.'

sewer but a bit of an old cow, she's certainly not in the audience.

What of Mr Vivian? That is how I referred to him and that is how I still think of him. A young man who was in his prime. A remarkably fine finisher; the best I've ever seen. He had so many interests outside of bookbinding. Lean and fit, he loved athletics and took part in many London to Brighton races. He enjoyed painting, fishing, golf and bedtime reading. He was rumoured to be a communist and a seller of the Daily Worker. I think of him as a radical who really cared about mankind. It's funny what you remember. He was one of three brothers and his dad built houses. Oh yes, and he supported Queen's Park Rangers. I went to the match with him sometimes even though I was a Brentford supporter.

Let me tell you a story of Mr Vivian. It happened in the bindery over 40 years ago. Many of you will remember the radio programme Housewives Choice. Housewives would write in to request their favourite music of the day, it was broadcast at 9 o'clock in the morning. The women sewers loved it. The BBC had guest presenters; one such was the famous bandleader Billy Cotton. It was said that he liked a good stiff drink and when he introduced the programme he was drunk. He introduced 'My Yiddisher Momma' by Sophie Tucker, but he didn't say Tucker. He slurred the word. The next day the newspapers were full of it. The first man to use the f... word on the radio! Mrs Hamilton thought it was a disgrace and swore he did say Tucker. Along with the sewers I enjoyed Housewives Choice.

Mr Vivian loved classical music on Radio 3. At first I hated it when he switched to the classical station, tuning into composer of the week. However he was in charge. He was a kindly boss and should be entitled to listen to the composer of the week occasionally. A piece of classical music had been playing for half an hour when Mr Vivian turned the volume right down and asked the sewers who had written the music. They were full of vulgar guesses. Mr Denham thought it was Beethoven. The antagonistic boy refused to answer. Instead, at Mr Denham's suggestion I wrote it down. The folded piece of paper was handed to Mr Vivian. He opened it slowly and to his amazement found I had got the right answer - Brahms Symphony No. 3. What he had not appreciated was that encouraged by his obvious love of music, I had begun to listen to as much classical music as I could. I too had fallen in love with it but I wasn't going to tell him that! Music is a very important part of my life. I hunger for it. Thank you Mr Vivian for introducing me to this great pleasure, and to your lovely Brahms.

Looking back on my apprenticeship, I was indeed most fortunate. I was encouraged to achieve only work of the highest standard. There was no pressure to knock off bindings for sale. They simply wanted me to be a fine craftsman. Let me go back to the beginning. I left school at 15 in 1959 and went to work in a leather factory in King's Cross. They dealt with cow hide - quality furniture leather fit for the House of Commons and Jaguar motor cars. My job was to make pattern books - little sample books. They sent me to the Central School to be taught blocking; gold embossed upon leather, it came quite easy to me. The blocking machine was part of the bookbinding department at the Central. I was allowed free of charge 4 evening classes a week and so I started bookbinding as an evening pleasure. Mr Knight, one of the tutors suggested a career in bookbinding. When I agreed, he arranged an interview at University College Library with the Chief Librarian, Joseph Scott and others whose names I can just about remember: Mrs Sanuba, Mr Gallagher and Mr Cabdebo.

I first met Mr Vivian with these distinguished people around a table, in a book lined room at the library. I must have made some impression because I accepted their invitation to become their first and only apprentice. So my short career at Connelly Brother's leather factory ended, and on a cold day

Mr Reginald Denham and Mr John Vivian at Flaxman House.

Apprenticeship served.

in February 1961 I started life as an impecunious apprentice bookbinder.

DAY 2: *June 25, a dull Llandudno day; rain at any moment.*

As Mr Vivian and his wife Lily lived with their two children only a ten minute walk from the Bindery, he was able to go home for lunch. We all envied him that, particularly the sewers. John and Lily lived above a chemists shop in Lambs Conduit Street. To make some pin money Lily helped with the making of various creams; pink for hands, white for the face and green for other parts. They were marketed under the label of Queens Cosmetics. I dare say there were many old queens floating about in Lamb's Conduit Street. Prominent people have lived there over the years including Charles Dickens and the veteran character actor of black and white British films Miles Malleson. This famous chemist shop had illustrious patrons such as Laurence Harvey and Gregory Peck. Mr Vivian did not lunch at home on Fridays as we had an in-bindery hot lunch, cooked by the men and the boy, but not by the sewers. We would take it in turns to cook but we were not allowed to repeat the dish. We started off with the simple stuff- beef stew, spaghetti bolognaise, liver 'n' bacon, casserole and so on. On one occasion it was Mr Vivian's turn to grace the Baby Belling. His dish was simmering away just as some visitors who had come to view the bindery were passing through. One of the visitors became alarmed at what he believed to be burning hot glue, not realising it was Mr Vivian's steak and potato casserole garnished with green cabbage. The sewers were highly amused. The hot Friday lunch continued for years. Mr Reginald Denham, the forwarder was once forced to add sardines to his spaghetti bolognaise; remember, we could not repeat dishes. I thought it was delicious - much better than Mr Vivian's glue dish.

Four times a year Messrs. Vivian, Denham and Delrue would go to Fleet Street - the home of the newspapers. There we would spend one hour on and one hour off gathering newspapers, tying them with string and throwing the bundles down the chute to be taken by van to the railway station. I hated the job, but it paid very well. There were many regulars in cloth caps who knew all the ropes. One toe - rag advised me not to give my real name when collecting the night's wages which could be as much as £14 which was a lot of money considering that the average weekly wage was about £12. I couldn't believe that the person in front of me had got his 14 quid having signed his chitty Mickey Mouse. In a panic I signed my name Vivian Denham. Hardly original, but it was all I could think of on the spur of the moment. John and Reg soldiered on for several years but I soon gave it up. It was not the life for me. Too many dodgy characters, and what do you do in London on a Sunday morning between finishing work at 4.00am and the first train home at 7. Sod the money!

I recall an occasion early on in my apprenticeship. Mr Vivian and Mr Denham decided to take me to see a musical; 'My Fair Lady', they said. I wasn't familiar with London. I took in the festive spirit as we walked through the Christmas lights of Soho. Hold on a moment. 'My Fair Lady', in Soho? With Messrs. Vivian and Denham laughing all the way, we ended up in Raymond's Revue Bar for a magical showing of 'My Bare Lady'. I became so engrossed I don't recall if there was any music. Sometime later I did see the proper show in Drury Lane with my sister Simone. An altogether different experience and dare I say not as exciting.

DAY 3: *July 2, a bright, sunny Wednesday after a dull, wet Tuesday.*

I wonder how many people knew Mr Vivian. It's not that he kept himself to himself. It's just that he had so many interests outside bookbinding and, of course, he had his family. He was trained as a finisher and was so outstanding he became a 'cock finisher'. There were just a few of them at the old W H Smith's Bindery in London. Their skill, discipline and dedication made them a breed apart. At University College, John Vivian was able to take in the complete range of skills both as forwarder and finisher. He had boundless enthusiasm for leather joints, double sewn silk headbands, edge gilding, leather covering, box making

Indenture of
Apprenticeship

BETWEEN

Paul Delrue

Mrs. Stephens

AND

Joseph W. Scott

Date commenced........27th February 1961

Date completed ....6 July 1965

BP 57

NORTH-WESTERN POLYTECHNIC
Prince of Wales Road NW5
Gulliver 1154

Principal SAUNDERS HARRIS B.COM. F.C.I.S. F.I.S.   *Head of Department* MALDWYN WILLIAMS

Report
from the Department of Printing
for the period ending 2 July 1965

P. C.

Student ___G. E. Delrue___   Course and Grade ___Craft Bookbinding___

Employer ___University College___

SUBJECT	TEACHERS' COMMENTS	INITIALS
Forwarding	*Excellent work on full leather extra binding*	R.E.P.
Finishing	*Further practice in tooling on full leather book, very good progress*	R.E.P.
Design	*Good, makes very good progress in design—*	V.M.E
Application to craft	*A very keen student with a clean and tidy approach.*	R.E.P.
Conduct	*Very Good.*	R.E.P.

DAY ATTENDANCE   out of

EVENING ATTENDANCE   out of

                     Maldwyn Williams

                     HEAD OF DEPARTMENT

and so on. These were all John's delights. I could not have asked for better mentors than Vivian and Denham. John could be a little untidy but he produced magic from clutter. I recall he used an old army vest to protect the book he was working on. As far as I could tell it was never washed and had a certain Middle Eastern odour, but one final polish and the books shone, crisp and bright. I'm sure the hierarchy in University College appreciated how fortunate they were to have such a unique talent. I left University College in the summer of 1971. Mr Vivian left soon after. He joined John Mitchell at the London College of Printing at Elephant and Castle. He proved to be an outstanding teacher; I met many of his students who, like me, appreciated his great skills and his ability to communicate.

As I come to the end of this talk recalling briefly the years I spent with my sensitive master, I can only express my gratitude that he, along with Reg, the sewers and the cleaner Mrs White gave me the warmest apprenticeship anyone could hope for. So, what has John left me? He has left me ever trying to achieve his fine standards. He has left me the memory of a thoroughly nice man, but it doesn't really end there. He gave me the first sounds I ever heard, the most beautiful sounds I ever heard; music. It travels with me always, even to Reading.

I hope I've made John smile in meeting him halfway to heaven, where I suspect he would give me a leg up, and we could listen together just once more to the sounds of music he so encouraged in me when I was such a boy.

(A speech given to the Society of Bookbinders Conference, Reading University 17-20 July 2003.)

Morgen

And tomorrow the sun will shine again,

And on the path that I shall take,

It will unite us,

Lucky ones again amid this sun breathing earth.

And to the beach, broad and blue waved,

We shall climb down, quiet and slow.

Speechless we shall gaze in each other's eyes,

And the speechless silence of happiness will fall on us.

Richard Strauss

Spring Sunday Morning Walk with Reg.

I am once again that small pale and ignorant youth of 16 years, first meeting Reg, he took me in, was my greatest friend. I learnt so much from him about life. He stirred my mind for the first time, gave me friendship, many walks, holidays, shared his small home at Leagrave for many years. It was my first real home, how I loved that little room at 109 Marsh Road. I enjoyed looking after myself for the first time. Cooking on my small baby belling, ironing shirts, looking good and smart for work at University College; my first real job with a future, hand bookbinding. Binding beautifully, the love of my life, I owe it all to him. He cared for me, brought the best out of me, made me complete.

Reg and Paul on a Barge Holiday 1963.

He was such a personality, loved by all. He introduced me to music and took me to concerts. At my unhappy home in Putney I had no future. Then along came Reg and Jean, who gave me so very much. I have many happy memories of Kilburn, the first real home I ever saw; carpets, records, books, stylish decorations, all that was fine and modern. What an impression it made on me as a teenager – I took it all in – even if I could not explain myself. I remember those early London walks on a Sunday and wish they could last forever. I might have joined the Army like so many of the boys who left the boys' home at fifteen. I was saved from all that.

I realise there are a few people you meet in life at the right time can make a difference. Reg was the ideal young man to befriend me. He was a perfect influence on me then and always. So much cheerful chatter and good humour, he was easy to get on with, sunny, warm and good fun. He was the perfect Best man at my wedding on that very cold March day in 1967.

'There was something in his face, That made me trust him at once.'

It seemed that he could do everything; decorating, electricity, plumbing, to make a home classy and beautiful. I always tried to copy him, but I had not quite the class or the material skill. I was some kind of artist and could bind books with some skill. I have loved bookbinding ever since. When he took charge of the bindery at University College in 1982, I visited him often – it was always a joy to keep in touch and meet the young sewers, or not so young; Rose Willett, Rose Hutton, Grace Mitchell and Mrs Hamilton. It was a happy place to visit. I always walked away with materials to help me out at my first Bindery in Leagrave.

146

I remember our Barge holiday on the Grand Union Canal! What a hard working holiday that turned out to be, but eventful nevertheless. I lost the lock key, was I in trouble then!

It was Reg and John Vivian who grew my musical seeds. I remember Reg suggesting I join The World Record Club, that wonderful treat where my classical musical ear first learnt to grow up. I still have those classical L.P.'s that Reg first introduced to me. Music goes so well with the long days on my own, binding books, my days with you and Reg come tumbling down. It's funny how music does that, evokes the past. In one of my early lunch breaks Reg took me to East Hampstead library, where I saw the great art bindings for the first time. I have never forgotten the quite beautiful, modern fine bindings and I told myself I will one day bind as beautifully, with colour and taste. Again with Reg, I went to my first ever London Bookbinding exhibition at Albermarle Street near Piccadilly. One of my books was shown and it won first prize as best apprentice binding. I owe all this to Reg. He kept my feet firmly on the ground, never letting me get too big for my boots, always modest and fair. I hope I made him proud.

He was loved and respected by everyone at University College, what a friend. I wonder what visitors thought with Reg and I wearing slippers all day long at the college – it was the thing we did – change into our slippers. He was a fine craftsman and I learnt more practical skills from him than any one else. He was a wonderful forwarder; could I ever match his skills? I have tried over the years. All those years walking together to Leagrave railway station and giving the regulars nicknames. He smiled at so many small instances; it made the journey much more acceptable.

Thank you Jean for knitting me all those warm pullovers and your bread and butter puddings were – and still are the best. Remember all those walks into Luton High Street? We must have been wonderfully fit in those days. Together we went into the estate agents where I brought my first ever house in Gardenia Avenue. I've now moved seven times ending at my present address at Ruthin. I have never had roots; it is the one thing I would have loved to have, family roots.

How Reg would have loved to walk with me in the Welsh countryside; meeting green hills, untouched as we walked for miles, fun and hard work along the way. The last time I saw Reg was when I lived in the City of Chester; it was wonderful to see him looking fit and well. He always cheered me up unlike anybody else, talking quickly, remembering the days and names of past places and the friends we grew up with in University College.

Reg and Jean.

Paul with Reg and Jeans daughter Sandra.

Over the years I have often talked of my early life with Reg and Jean. You both made such an impact. Now I look back, remembering my theatre days when we saw Tony Newley in 'Stop the World I Want to Get Off' at The Queen's in Shaftesbury Avenue. How I'd like to stop the world for a single day and take a spring Sunday morning walk with Reg, talking very little, just being with each other. A person such as Reg should be living into old age and continuing to give all that meet him a few joyful words. We shall all miss him and for me a bright light has dimmed, but only for a moment. After all he influenced me, wherever I go along the way of life you'll both be with me. Jean, you were his perfect partner. What more could you want and ask – just one more day?

The Apprentice Years.

It was my first entry into the world of the bookbinding competition. The competition was known as 'The Harrison' and in 1963 I entered my book of 'Rudyard Kipling's Collected Verse' into Class B Students. This was for apprentices up to the age of 21. I had just turned 18 and I wondered if I was the youngest apprentice to enter. The following year, 1964, I was successful and won the best apprentice prize of £15.00 donated by Major J R Abbey. I was surprised and quietly delighted; it pleased my teachers at the Central. The 'sixties' were successful and in 1965 I was commended with my book 'The Face of Ancient China'. The last binding worked on by George Frewin.

I had just turned twenty-one and went up to Class A (students up to the age of twenty-six), where I entered my book entitled 'English Insects'. Mr Bernard Middleton was lucky for me, he was one of the judges in the sixties and that was it. I entered books throughout the seventies and eighties but I was never quite as successful. In 1990 the bookbinding competition changed, there were many more prizes and the Folio Society became involved. They donated the prize money and also printed the sheets for the 'set book' category. This gave the judges a chance to compare different approaches to the same book. They continued the 'open choice' category, which brought more fun to the proceedings and the number of prizes continued growing.

In 1990 I bound two books, the 'set book' and the 'open choice'. The set book was entitled 'Poems of War' and my open choice was 'Zaehnsdorfs'. My Books received first prize. I had not been successful for years and finally I made it. That was it, my last Harrison entry. Of course I missed it over the years (the barren years). I always enjoyed putting my books in, and when I compared mine with others, I was surprised I did so well. Since 1963 I have entered twenty bindings and won the

'I have always wanted to ask the sky and the trees what they think of me...'

'...Are they whispering to the almighty Gods?'

most important prize; 'The Best Apprentice for the Year 1964'. I bound 'Headhunters' when I was nineteen. Still, after all these years it is the prize I value above all others, for the first time I was judged on a talent I hardly knew I had.

Many thanks go to my teachers in those apprentice years. Mr Fred Wood, George Frewin and the Designer Bookbinders all inspired me. I always had a free mind and the great craftsmen were behind me. Could I ever put into practice what I see in my mind, and lay it down onto the book covers? I still feel rather sad for the many bookbinders who have never been prize winners; after all, they bind their level best, putting in as many hours as me. It is easy to say there have to be winners and losers, but it still makes me uneasy. To all the unsuccessful bookbinders and students, I salute you. You have all given me much pleasure.

I still enjoy binding as I did all those years ago. My first Design Binding, in 1959, was called 'Happy England'. I was an

'Happy England', bound in 1959. My first design binding, age 15.

evening class student, at the Central in London and had just left secondary school in Enfield, North London. I was fifteen and had a natural feel for hand binding. My love for the craft continued to grow and in 1960 I completed a Holy Bible with a cover design which was unusual for the time; a distinct departure from tradition. The first ever beautiful fine leather binding I saw as an evening class pupil was by John Collins, bound in Crimson goatskin. It was a large binding which had been decorated with a gold and black linear design. I was suddenly taken aback. How I wished I could be so talented, but I had no design skills, I never went to Art School, where do you begin? It takes time and time was what I had. I looked around and saw my imagination rise. I realised I seemed to look differently at almost everything. I could not wait to seriously start on my first book. I had doubts and wondered if I had taken on too much. I looked at bindings by other students, but I was not inspired until I saw the magical bindings of this group of people calling themselves 'Designer Bookbinders', could I ever be part of this untouchable group?

The Ninth Annual Competition.
Kentish Town, London 1965.

George Frewin looking on.

My Student Entry binding was 'The Face of Ancient China' and was bound in silver grey Oasis Morocco leather, onlayed in blue goatskin with gold tooling and gilt edges. In some ways, this binding was a turning point in my career, and certainly the most difficult to date. It was a large, square book, full of illustrations and forwarded, as usual, with leather joints. George Frewin's keenness to be involved in the design delayed the work for some months, leaving me time to practice my gold tooling. I was using gouges for the first time; it seemed slow work and I was beginning to feel frustrated as there is only so much practice to be done, before losing interest. Mr Frewin just did not turn up.

I arrived at Friday Day Classes promptly at 9am, Mr Wood was already there and waiting for me. He invited me into his office as, under my breath, I bemoaned the fact that Mr Frewin was not there;

"Will I ever finish China?"

Mr Wood told me to sit down and passed me a large white envelope with my name, full title of the competition book, and the words, 'Design for Delrue'. Mr Frewin's son had passed the envelope on to Mr Wood. George Frewin had just died, and the envelope had been propped up by his bedside.

'I fear only the unforgiving.'

I was trembling with shock, hearing the news in such a way. Mr Wood said nothing as he passed me the envelope. Pale faced, I left the office and walked alone for several hours around the streets of Kentish Town, downcast. How could I have been so selfish? Thinking only of myself and my binding, while Mr Frewin lay dying. I broke down; relieved I was on my own. A great craftsman was dead and working on my book, 'The Face of Ancient China' 'til his end.

It began to rain, but I hardly noticed as I turned to go back to classes. The other students and apprentices said little but smiled in sympathy. Lying on the bench was the sealed envelope, which Fred Wood opened, taking out the last designs of George Frewin, for my book.

154

"It must be our best book. We must bind in his memory." Mr Wood simply said.

And so it was. The best I could manage and the loveliest. During the many months I spent on it, I somehow sensed the face of George Frewin looking down and willing me on. Even now, I know it was a most difficult binding and that it got the very best out of me. I was still an apprentice, I felt the loss of George Frewin very deeply and acknowledged that this had been the last book of a remarkable craftsman.

I was truly privileged to have such a fine teacher to live up to. I don't know if I have done so, but I have tried.

Bookbinding and Beyond.

I have often been asked to write about bookbinding and how I have made a living by it, especially now that I have been binding for fifty years. My first thoughts are once again in St Joseph's Boys' Home, in Enfield. It was there that Mr Ron Arbetta ran craft evenings and singled me out to make a pair of white kid gloves to go on show at The National Association of Boys' Clubs. I gained a First Class Art Festival award with them (for leather work) in May 1959. I was fourteen years old and the thrill was so great that when the Sisters of Charity asked me what I would like to do when I left the home in the summer of 1959, I said I would like to work making gloves. I was taken to Connolly Brothers Curriers, at King's Cross, a leather factory that made furniture to be covered in cow-hide; I never got to make another pair of white kid gloves.

I often wonder why Mr Ron Arbetta had singled me out from amongst the two hundred other boys and what he had seen in me. He was a slight man, always in a suit, who had a friendly manner although he rarely smiled. With a sharp nose, milky complexion and beautiful hands, he worked magic in front of me and the other boys. When I left the home I never saw him again, but I remember him clearly. There was a sadness about him because perhaps he knew that outside St Joseph's, there was little going for us boys. Our schooling was inadequate. All we were good at was sport; football and table tennis, but with no preparation to help us get a worthwhile job with prospects. We never thought about the future.

I was just fifteen when I went to work in the leather factory. Mr Robinson, the Works Manager, arranged for me to work on the top floor, well away from the 'regulars'. I worked in the pattern department making leather sample books to be sent out to customers, but they wanted gold decoration on the covers and so I was asked to attend the Central School of Arts and Crafts in Holborn to learn to use a blocking machine. I was given day release on Tuesdays and Fridays, blocking gold foil all day long.

It was an important turning point in my life, as I met the people who would guide me to a worthwhile career.

Life has its twists and turns and I found myself moving towards a craft I knew very little about; a world of books, learning and discovery. I could hardly read or write; I was good at handwork but in need of help and understanding. At this point I was living with my family in Putney, always feeling in the way and deeply unhappy. I had a fear of adults and saw no future for myself other than joining the Army, like so many of the other boys from the home. My time at the college felt like the security of St Joseph's. I enjoyed the day release classes and the teachers liked me, for I was naturally polite and well mannered. One of the teachers, Mr Knight, invited me to attend the evening classes that my day release entitled me to. So, I became a gold blocker during the day and bookbinding student at night. Six months later Mr Knight asked me if I would like to become an apprentice bookbinder with University College, London. I became tearful and a little frightened at that point. All my experiences of life up until then had been letdowns and disappointments. I trusted no one, keeping to myself and rarely smiling; I was not at ease with life.

My first experience of Christmas outside the Home had been tramping the streets of Putney, sheltering in doorways. My mother told me that my step-father's elderly parents were coming to spend Christmas with them and since they knew nothing of me, I would be expected to make myself scarce! I was bewildered with the thought that every Christmas might have to be like that. How long would I have to be hidden away? Did this happen to all the boys from St Joseph's? I became withdrawn, truly unhappy and lonely.

Mr Knight let me be as I packed up my few bookbinding tools ready to leave. He spoke kindly and softly, telling me not to worry, that the apprenticeship position could be held for another week. Then he asked me if I lived at home with my father. I held myself together for as long as I could before the tears began to flow unchecked. He held my hand and I was able to tell him that I had no father but lived in my mother's rented flat with my step-father and small brother Norman. I felt better for telling him and he worked hard to get the apprenticeship at University College for me. I had to fight my over sensitive nature, but I was determined to lead a useful life.

In February 1961 I was taken on as an apprentice at University College London, a boys' home boy with a real future. At seventeen years of age I was able to leave that Putney house and feel real happiness for the first time. The teachers at the Central School had played a big part in my life; for the first time I had friends who were interested in me and, even better, I found that Bookbinding came easily to me. I loved it.

As I grew up I discovered myself and my talents emerged; a gift with my hands, a musical ear and the feeling that I had something to say, although at that time I still found it difficult to express myself. I found that I could make people laugh and for the first time in my life I was listened to. At the house in Putney I had been considered 'dopey and thick,' just a nuisance, and in the way. But Bookbinding released the real me and my hands were at last put to practical and creative use. At University College Bindery, Gower Street, London I was on my way in the world and spent ten happy years there. At the bindery there were sewers, forwarders, a finisher and the apprentice, me.

I was the only apprentice they ever took on and what an experience it was, meeting different kinds of binders who, like me, had served as apprentices of the 'old school.' I worked on regular binding, repeating skill after skill, a variety of work from buckram to leather, rebacks to repairs, box making to simple finishing, raised bands, leather labels, sewn headbands, polishing full leather bindings, rounding and backing and so on, but of my great love, design bindings, there were none. I worked on these during my day release day on Fridays under Mr George Frewin, Fred Woods and Jim Parks, with Les Knight in the evenings. The same Mr Knight who first understood me and handed me the apprenticeship at University college. I shall always be thankful to him, even now the pain of those early years is still with me; he was a father figure.

My day release Friday was under the best craftsman I have ever practiced with; Mr Fred Wood. He held me spell bound with his natural skills and could do the lot. The magic of his hands as he covered the first full leather book I ever saw, his beautiful headcaps. I never saw him bully the leather, he used his hands to mould the leather round the boards, spot on corners, pure poetry. If only I could do that one day, relax and bind easily and beautifully, but I did notice his bright eyes, his seriousness and felt at once that he had practised and honed his bookbinding skills over many years.

He and George Frewin were to teach together for twenty years – what a partnership. To give him his full name; Frederick Louis Wood (nicknamed 'Woody' amongst the apprentices) gained a trade scholarship to Central School of Arts and Crafts in 1933 studying under Peter McLeish. It was after the war he taught at Central School with George Frewin helping to set up the fine binding section at Watford College and finally lecturing at Camberwell School of Art. How lucky I was to have the best years with him.

My first ever full leather, design binding at the Central School, 'Happy England' was bound with my evening class tutors George Frewin and Fred Wood. The leather I used (a crimson cowhide), I had acquired from the leather factory where I worked. The book had raised bands, a leather label, hand lettered title and all gilt edges. I made a slip case for it and was charged four shillings for the materials. I kept that book with me, before giving it away as a birthday gift to a young friend. It was bound while I was still working at Connolly's and it was the lettering that gave me the most difficulty. I made label after label until I was reasonably happy with it. Even so, I felt could have done better with it, until my master said;

"Delrue, this really is the best you can do, and far better than the much older boys!"

The second binding was a small Holy Bible, bound in full dark green, with a simple gold cross on the front cover; my first true design binding and destined to become an early favourite. I gave it to my grandmother and she was thrilled. Some years later on seeing the book again, I realised that I had put her initials on the spine of the book , 'V.D.' for Violette Delrue. I had always wondered what had made the apprentices laugh. She had been the only family member to show any interest in my bookbinding, this strange occupation that kept me going, made me happy and excited me. She gave me support in my work. Years later she died with my Bible in her hands, and after it was returned to me. On the flyleaf I had written:

For Grandmother at Christmas 1961,
You believed in me,
Your loving Grandson Paul.

I was now ready and eager to please my new bookbinding teachers with a design book. My opportunity came in the form of 'Rudyard Kipling's Collected Verse'. It was entered for the Thomas Harrison Memorial Competition for Students and Apprentices, in 1963. There were just three prizes and I was not so lucky, but my masters told me I had made a good account of myself and I entered again, the following year, with a binding of the 'Head Hunters of Papua New Guinea'. This time I secured the first prize for Best Apprentice and my prize was £15.00, donated by a Major J R Abbey.

The exhibition of competition prize winners was to be held at the National Book Leagues building near Green Park. I went alone to the prize giving, but I did meet the friendly faces of Mr Wood and his beautiful wife, who put me immediately at my ease. She said her husband had spoken of his new star pupil Mr Delrue often at the breakfast table, adding:

"Now I can put a face to the name. Pleased to meet you, young Paul and best of luck!"

I was shaking with fear, not wanting my name to be called, all of my old insecurities came rushing out. I wished to be far away from all these seemingly 'posh' people. Eventually my name was called and I went forward to collect my envelope; at last, I had proved that I was not the 'thickhead' my family had believed me to be, but I could bind as beautifully as those before me.

In binding 'Head Hunters' I had used highlights of white kid, provided by the evening gloves of George Frewin's wife, an opera lover it seemed. Indeed, I was going the opera way myself; classical music was beginning to take hold. I was particularly moved by the music of the Frederick Delius opera, 'A Village Romeo and Juliet'. It was almost unbearably beautiful; it held me breathless. How could anyone put such sounds down on paper? How could anyone convey these feelings that were beginning to take me over? It was a miracle. At just eighteen and only three years out of St Joseph's Boys' Home, I fell in love with English music and felt a part of it.

The '60s were a good time for me. I continued with further Harrison competition successes. Bookbinding was beginning to take a hold over me and though I had an inkling of the quality of my work I preferred to let the books do the talking. Even after so many years it is difficult for me to acknowledge compliments. I find it hard just to say thank you and smile nicely. On reaching the age of twenty-one I came out of my apprentice time, but continued evening classes, as I still thought there was much more to learn and practice. I discovered I could help others with things like head banding and gold tooling, fellow students found me a friendly face and always seemed pleased to see me. Nice old ladies brought in 'goodies' such as cakes and fudge, a bagful to share among my hard-up bookbinding friends, toe-rags the lot of them! I had been completely overcome; music and bookbinding, the greatest loves of my life I could never do without! How could this be? Why me?

Prelude to a Kiss.

It was the first time my apprentice had been to a country house, surrounded by gardens and comforts. I was to give a long weekend bookbinding course to people that had never bound a book, but want to have a go. There were twenty students, mostly of retirement age perhaps, they were keen and willing; what more could you ask? My apprentice and I arrived early Friday afternoon, setting out the bookbinding tools and materials. My first job was to put on my tape of classical music, just to relax me before the onslaught, the arrival of the students, all mad keen and raring to go. There were many comings and goings, the weekend was going to be busy and I must pace myself; but at least my apprentice was there to help. It was his first posh bookbinding weekend.

The class continued until we heard the gong for the much looked forward to evening meal. The food was plentiful and good, with much variety. Our long table was soon full with eager students, eating and talking in excited measure. The last student to take a seat? Well, let me describe him: I was uncomfortable even to look at him. He was about sixty-ish, tall, but the face, I had never seen anything like it. A large head, hairy thing, large bulging eyes with red circles, a long face, with his front tooth resting on his lower lip. His lips were wide and he had cheekbones that stood out. He had a long neck and hands so big it was frightening. I could barely look at him, and to think I was to spend a weekend bookbinding with this freak of nature. He came up to me and with a slight accent introduced himself.

"I'm George and I'm so looking forward to binding my small notebook with you."

I barely looked up, but I was able to thank him, as uncomfortable as I felt.

"What are we going to do with Big George"? I said to my apprentice later.

Please help me out someone! At least there were others around me to protect me and keep my distance from George. I wish I could called it a day and return to my bindery in dear old Chester, but I must make a go of it. I cannot let the other students down. And so our weekend course began with George at the back of the class (thank God). We all worked well together. As always there was much fun and laughter, folding of paper, sewing, endpapering, rounding, lining up the spine, headbands and the luxury of coloured ribbon markers; what a start!

Some were quite good with their hands and others indifferent, but poor old George was hopeless, he found it difficult to thread a needle, so my apprentice and I kept an eye on him, helping out and giving him more attention. He had a way of mocking himself and very much joining in. Even though he was lagging behind the others, he kept a good sense of proportion and smiled a lot. It was when he stood up that, for the first time, I noticed his very big feet. He was just like a walking circus clown without the makeup. But for all his faults he remained cheerful, I was amazed. We were all getting use to George and kept him as part of our bookbinding circle. We all went as usual for our coffee break, but no George. I said to my apprentice;

'He is not sensitive to the feelings of others, and far too sensitive to his own feelings.'

162

"Return if you please and see if George has lost his way or something."

He returned to the Dining room saying that George was sweeping and tidying up the room to be ready for our return. I excused myself, I will be back in a moment.

"George, do you want to do someone out of a job, they have cleaners here, will you come and join us for coffee?" I asked. He looked up and smiled;

"Yes Sir, at Once."

"Thank you George." I replied

So we, or I was getting used to George. I felt sure that he felt left out and I was beginning to feel bad about myself.

"George, have you travelled far to be here? What do you do for a living?" I inquired.

"Well Paul, I am a Policeman and I live and work in my native Liverpool. I live with my dear old Mum and have done so all my life. I simply love my job and it is the only job I have ever had – but don't worry, I don't walk the beat. I don't wish to frighten people."

I began to be with and talk freely with George. He even bought me a drink to finish our first full and big day; we had started at nine and finished at nine in the evening. I certainly needed that glass of house red. Tomorrow we were going to title the note books in gold along the spine so I had to be clear headed, for I told all the students:

"Now is the time for originality; I don't want 'cooking' or 'gardening notes', but interesting and thoughtful titles. Sleep on it overnight, something like 'Limnor' to be getting on with; it means study of pond life – that's a start."

163

'His mind has gone, poor man, He sang and laughed the whole way there, I never saw him so happy and so free from care.'

After a comfortably night's sleep and a lazy breakfast we were all having a go at finishing.

"...or, if you don't want to spoil your little book just watch me and pass me the hand letters."

They all wisely passed me the hand letters. They had come up with wonderful titles. I was thrilled. Someone had thought up 'My first book with Delrue' I liked that, but felt a bit embarrassed. I had real arm ache but my young apprentice showed us all what he was made of and helped to title many of the books. So, all went well until it came to George.

"Paul, I noticed right from the beginning you love classical music, you relax to it remember? So I would like to call my book 'PRELUDE', a musical term made out of your name P Delrue."

I was cut short at George's response – the loveliest thing that ever happened. George passed me each letter and although the book was a little 'woolly' the title came out beautifully.

"Paul, you must now keep my book as it has your name on it and it will remind you of our most enjoyable weekend bookbinding course."

We all went into the dining room and had out last meal (a hot roast) before we departed for home. George helped me load the car with our bookbinding bits and pieces, wooden presses and so on. My apprentice was already sitting in the car having already said goodbye to George and the rest of the happy students. I walked nervously towards George, looked him squarely in the eyes, held his hands tightly and thanked him for making the bookbinding weekend such a success. He smiled at me and said:

"I have lived with my face and have learned to live with what I have, it's a bit of a fright, but that's life."

I handed George a notebook that I had kept secret from the Students. It was made by my apprentice and myself with the title in gold. Its title I will keep to myself, it could never match up to George's 'PRELUDE' that's for sure. There has been much soul searching over the years, remembering a face of beauty, understanding and kindness that you rarely meet.

164

Finding a Voice. *An interview.*

Recognising your undoubted artistic skill, how has it developed from having had no formal art training?

"That's a question which I would have been unable to answer until a couple of years ago, because, until then I didn't feel I had anything individual to offer - technical skill maybe but artistic skill?

I have made very slow progress since 1961, sound technical ability providing a form of confidence but a traditional apprenticeship at University College, London imprinted bookbinding but artistic influence was absent. I do remember noticing posters in the Underground, film advertising in particular, colour, design and typography with foreign films having the most seductive graphic art style. Even now, when visiting London, posters, especially for exhibitions, provide ideas.

In the time which followed - the best part of twenty years - my annual entry in the Thomas Harrison annual competition depended heavily on those practical skills. For instance I used leather onlay to reproduce pictorial designs.

I am always more at ease with flowing rather than straight lines. Nowadays my bindings develop spontaneously, almost in an organic way as opposed to the traditional method when the thinking process is finalised off the book.

I seem to have invented my own expressive collection of ideas, which possibly would not have benefited from a formal art training."

What has been the strongest influence or inspiration in your binding?

"Examining fine buildings in detail, the designs in particular, I have come to realise it has been the technical

165

bookbinding skill of Fellows of DB which has most impressed and inspired me."

How does the text or the contents of the book influence your design choice?

"I am inspired by both words and illustrations and respond to texts with a serious moral theme. Some I am intimate with more or less straight away. For years I have had a love hate relationship with the Bible. Social statements draw me. I do not have that rather precious academic communication with a text but respond emotionally."

Having established a basis for design - do you first see it in form, or in colour?

"Shape first. I remember though, working on 'The Pity of War.' The design came so slowly, I was trying too hard and working too hard on how to apply my own skills. Once I concentrated on my feelings about war, ideas developed from my emotional reaction to the text - huge wrongs, the atrocities, never the glory of war."

What are your views on mixed materials such as metals, wood, plastics?

"As a small boy I was happiest with soft things, a woollen blanket, a pair of leather gloves, soft and malleable. I remember old 78's could be moulded after immersing in boiling water, fascinating. I have never been drawn to hard surfaces. There are wonderful examples by binders which I do admire, who use metals, plastics etc but these are materials which require more pre-planning than the way I like to work."

Has your artistry developed in other spheres outside bookbinding?

"I have a 'musical soul'. Music is the strongest influence

on my life. Other people may work best in peace and quiet but my most creative working environment is provided by a blend of music and binding, gently punctuated by the right visitor at the right time. The bindery atmosphere is vital, some seem almost clinical to my taste."

In the aspiring bookbinder what qualities or skills would you look for and consider most important?

"A trainee must be neat and clean. I look for a quiet dedication, the realisation of a modest outlook. There must undoubtedly be enthusiasm and a natural feeling for the craft, sitting or standing for certain jobs, a balance of the body. There must be patience and dedication with attention to detail, and of course, someone who is not looking to make money. All in all, a very rare individual."

Looking to the future, how do you see the designer's approach to bookbinding changing?

"The developments I foresee are divorced from the craft of bookbinding. The skill of binding will become less important, sculptural form taking priority, visible in the developing importance of 'containers'. Binding will become the art form and the book will be a subsidiary element. I do feel those designers will be missing out, bookbinding has so much to offer. It must be remembered that there is beauty in the feel of a binding. It must open well and function as intended, what is placed upon it will be unique but should not take over from the original concept."

Can you tell me a little of your most recent binding?

"I have been invited to take part in Designer Bookbinder's project which commemorates the centenary of the Tregaskis Exhibition of seventy three binders interpretation of William Morris's 'King Florus and the Fair Jehane'. The subject is Andrew Marvel's 'The Garden & Other Poems' published by The Folio Society, originally covered in black silk with a gold card slip case.

In a single section, which I wanted to make more substantial, it provided the perfect opportunity to create a binding which satisfied exactly the pleasures of a small book; opening well, fitting snugly in the hand and not excessively decorated.

My approach was to introduce a little colour inside the book and just a touch on the cover. The Brockway engravings were inspirational and random-marbled paper guards (which had to be lightweight) were carefully selected to reflect the form and emotion of each page. Covers and doublures are of naturally marked suede with fissures allowing a flash of brilliant yellow to shine through."

Taken from the Society of Bookbinders journal, 1987.

What Makes a Good Teacher?

Since I was fifteen years old under the eye of the Teachers of Bookbinding at the Central School, George Frewin and Fred Woods, I have felt that one day, I would very much like to teach. But what skills would I need? I struggle to explain things, I doubt myself and lack confidence. But I truly want to share my love of bookbinding.

When I became an apprentice at University College I was given day release at the Central, meeting for the first time the older 'trade boys' who had to work differently to me. I was a hand bookbinder. I practiced hand skills, but the older boys mostly worked in machine shops, where variety was scarce. I was lucky to be at the College bindery. I was their first ever apprentice and in those days, a 'Forwarder'. On my Friday day release at The Central, I became a designer bookbinder. Working on one book a year in full leather, I was allowed to explore a wide range of techniques and skills, coloured onlays, or inlays, gold decoration, hand lettering, design work, gilt edges, silk sewn headbands, leather joints and doublures, mixed coloured end-papers, sewing on card and on tape and box making. I also gained experience working with goatskin, vellum, calf and strange animal skins, nothing seemed beyond my teachers.

I feel my ability to communicate is somehow inadequate when trying to convey the complexities and subtleties of creating. How I have managed to pass on my skills to my apprentices I cannot say, but I have tried. I could never match up to the golden years at the Central School under Frewin and Wood, with Les Knight in the evenings.

'I shall not see their likes.' My first go at teaching was taking over from Lou Smith, for one evening only, at the Stanhope Institute in London. Then later, at the Luton College of Art, I took over from Tony Cains for a couple of years, two evenings a week. In those days we had to have sixteen pupils to allow classes even to start. It was

a lot of hard work, but I loved it and gained in confidence. I found that the pupils liked me and we had a lot of fun, but I was strict with work. I never told anyone off, though some were awful, no, terrible. They never made mistakes other than being 'indiscrete', as I would say. I felt sad for the people who had little in the way of hand skills, but had unfailing enthusiasm and endless energy. The students were above all great company. I learnt such a lot in my Luton teaching days, even how to pare buffalo or kangaroo leather! What more could you want?

'Life is all about what might have been.'

My favourite memory of a student from my Luton days was of a merchant banker who insisted on using a French paring knife. Having 'gone through' the leather in a major way he changed his mind from doing a full leather binding and decided on two half leathers instead. Thankfully the French paring knife was never seen again. Is it still in his posh office in London I wonder?

170

All in all, in my fifty years of bookbinding I have probably taught hundreds of private pupils, often for free and can safely say I have made very little, if any money from it. That may have been part of the pleasure. We have all taken something from our time together; fun, companionship and bookbinding.

So what do I think makes a good teacher? You must understand failure, have a sense of humour, suffer disappointment with most students, but understand their faults, smile, be on hand to help and have bags of enthusiasm. Remember, there will be somewhere out there, a golden nugget that will stay with you year after year, and you will remember how you helped them along the way. For me, I feel the disappointment of my failures, for I am too demanding. I expect too much from students and myself. I am always searching for another 'Delrue' a boy with a little magic in his hands, just like those of George Frewin and Fred Wood.

Ruthin Craft Centre, 1981.

It happened years ago when I was working at the New Ruthin Craft Centre. The craftsmen were looking forward to the first ever Summer Bank Holiday, where we would be meeting the public, and there was a holiday festival air about the place.

The Craft Centre at Ruthin was the first purpose-built complex of its kind in Wales. It was built round an attractive courtyard where traditional skills could be practised in a public forum. The centre housed fourteen craft studios which were occupied by independent craft workers, demonstrating and talking about their skills. The courtyard featured a sunken podium for summer programmes of outdoors events and children's theatre productions. There was also a restaurant serving simple meals and snacks. It had views from every side; the pastoral Vale of Clwyd and the mountains and moors of North Wales. It seemed like the ideal setting to bring the craft of bookbinding to the attention of the people of Wales.

Recently, I had bound a presentation copy of 'The Bilingual New Testament' to be presented to Prince Charles and Lady Diana Spencer on the occasion of their wedding, which felt like a head start. I decided to do a flashy demonstration of gold leaf finishing, since I knew that bookbinding can look rather slow and uninteresting to the ordinary public.

The doors opened and coach loads of people poured into the centre to watch, learn and buy. At that moment I was thinking of all the books I would be given to repair or rebind, added to that all the bound artists' notebooks and albums I would sell, tastefully decorated with my own marbled paper. Passing trade, for the first time!

But people were not interested in bookbinding and my new studios did not set the public alight. At the other workshops, crowds were queuing to see carved candles, stained glass, pottery, frame making, calligraphy, furniture and French polishing, but poor old Bookbinding was 'on the shelf'. I was left alone, saddened and slightly embarrassed. Still, I was not to be interrupted with my real gold-leaf finishing. All the noise and clamour seemed to belong to another world; all was peaceful and calm within my Ruthin Craft Centre Bindery. Many hours went by until at last I heard the sound of knocking at my new, red painted studio door. A womans voice was saying:

"Bookbinding? That's boring but you can go in if you like. I'm going to look at the other crafts and treat myself to a nice cup of tea. See you in a couple of hours, or sooner, if you lose interest."

In walked a shy boy dressed in a grey and navy school uniform. Not knowing where to start, I beckoned him nearer my workbench. I was laying on gold over the leather spine, waiting for the tools to heat up. Silently he watched, spellbound, as I picked up the letters, cooled them down and applied them to the spine, adding lines and a decorative motif.

'Perhaps he has secrets for changing life?'

Finally, I used the gold rubber to remove the excess gold and the work stood out, bright and clear. I took the volume out of the press and showed it to the boy, offering it up for him to hold.

The first bindery in Ruthin.

He gently ran his fingers over the spine, polished leather and raised bands.

"How do you do that?" were his first words, his clear eyes gleaming. I asked him his name and how far he had travelled.

"My name's Philip, my Mum brought me. She gets impatient but I love books and reading more than the TV. We travelled down from Blackpool to stay with my auntie in Ruthin."

"How old are you Philip?" I asked.

"Nearly thirteen." he replied.

"Fetch yourself one of my notebooks, Philip. Together we shall put your name on it and decorate the book. I love the old craft and you have shown interest in it, so I'd like to give you one of my books."

Philip chose a nice plain note book and brought it round to my side of the bench where he picked out the letters for his name and carefully placed them on the stove. Having warned him not to touch the hot stove, he handed me the letters one by one as I tooled in his name, adding gold lines top and bottom. When I rubbed away the excess gold and then took it out of the finishing press, he gave me a big wide smile.

'I must be in a hurry, Not waste a single day, The wind rushes on and the soft brown leaves fall...'

"Shall we go for a little bit more excitement with gold decorations on the boards?" I asked.

His eyes gleamed as I tooled in gold lines and stars; the little book looked alive and was a beauty.

174

"Philip, this is yours. Would you like me to show you how I put the gold on from this book of gold leaf?"

I showed him how to take the leaf with my knife and place it on the cushion pad, before cutting it to size. Philip greased the spine and laid on the gold leaf beautifully and successfully, first time. He reminded me of myself as a young apprentice.

'...Only to be crushed underfoot, By the mindless lives of the living.'

Neither of us had noticed that by this time other people had entered the bindery, and in fact it was now quite full. I ran the wheel along the front cover and Philip used the gold rubber gently and surprisingly well. Slowly the bindery emptied and we were again left to ourselves.

I showed Philip other bindings, including 'The Bilingual New Testament' to be given to the young couple the following Thursday. I had not hidden it and, in fact, Philip was the only other person to see and handle it. He was thrilled. His mother called in, surprised that the boy was still there.

"Well, Philip, we must be off. It's almost closing time and auntie expects us at 6 o'clock, remember! Now thank Mr Delrue and remember your manners. I hope he hasn't been a nuisance."

The boy looked forlorn and, not saying a word, he left slowly, his mother closing the door quietly behind them. I never saw Philip again.

I have often wondered what became of him and if he remembered his summer Bank Holiday afternoon with the Bookbinder, at Ruthin Craft Centre. It was memorable for me, with his eager face, many questions and enthusiasm for all that I showed him. I often ask myself:

"What is the future of the craft I love?"

In the hands of young Philip, who lives with his mum in Blackpool, perhaps?

Reflections of a Golden Eye.

In remembering Sally Lou Smith my story goes back to the early '60s. Out of all the Fellows of Designer Bookbinders she was simply the best, I came to seek her approval above all. In 1962 I saw for the first time her beautiful design bindings in her West Hampstead library. I'd never seen anything like it, either at University College London where I was an apprentice or Central School, Southampton Road, Kingsway. It was all new to me.

Lou Smith lived, in those days, in Camden Town. I paid her a visit during my lunch break, meeting her for the first time. She answered the door, looked at me and said she could give me a few minutes. I had telephoned first out of good manners, to arrange a meeting. She was uncomfortable, I felt it and wished I hadn't come, but it was too late, I was shy and awkward. She led the way into the front room, her bindery, but said very little, I said nothing. She was polite and showed me her latest book, but this I cannot remember. I took nothing in. I wanted to get out and after a very long five minutes or so, relieved, she opened the front door and I was quickly let out. That was my first meeting with her. I could not reconcile such beauty in her bindings, with this tall elegant American lady, wearing glasses. I never went there again -ever- but I still loved her work.

Paul and Sally Lou Smith.

I looked forward to the Thomas Harrison Memorial competition, when her bindings would be on show. 'Trial of the Poet', 'Trois Contes' and 'In Search of India' were some of the titles I recall. She always seemed (rightly) to win and her bindings always stayed with me. She clearly had the best eye in the business - *a Golden Eye.* I read all that she wrote and visited Designer Bookbinder's exhibitions over the years. It was her books I made a direct line for. I was not comfortable with her but always loved her work.

I applied rather nervously for Fellowship of Designer Bookbinders some years ago. I was not selected. After all, how could I match up to these Bookbinding Gods even after all these years? I had been around for almost 30 years; it saddened me. I decided to write to Lou Smith, to ask for help. She replied to me, but her letter was rather matter of fact and not really helpful. The Camden Town Story all over again, but I was a 16 year old boy then; now I had been hanging around for years and still no approval from the Golden Eye, was it ever to be? I applied again the following year and was let in. I had become a tired old God of bookbinding, but happy to be there. I love the world of beautiful bindings and I at last had made it. I even gave a talk about my work entitled 'Bookbinding and influences - 42 years on' at the Queen Square, London. I hardly set the world alight and few people came (I'm not big in London!). I should have invited friends and family to bulk up the pews, but never mind. I did recognise some faces, and there was always tea to look forward to at the end. We all had to make way for Lou Smith and her wheel chair. I made myself thin, so she could pass to reach the tea and biscuits, but her beeline was for me. I remember very clearly, in her American lilt she said:

"Paul, since the 'Harrison' days I have always kept an eye on you, always. You had overdone the technique too much, keep it simple, remember space can be beautiful, now you leave space and have done for years. You have always been one of my favourite bookbinders. I love your work."

Lou Smith had given me what I always wanted, her approval of my work, I only hope I can match up to it in the years to come. I shall surely miss her elegant original and beautifully bound books that have given me many golden years of pleasure looking out for her work, quite unlike anyone else's. A remarkable American craftsman, who I first met in Camden Town nearly 50 years ago.

Remembering John Coleman:
The Founder of the Society of Bookbinders.

My memory can never be in facts or figures. When John Coleman left school in the 1920s he decided not to take up the offer to be a schoolboy international footballer, or to be signed up by Bristol City. Instead, John's first job was at the jewellers in his home town of Bath, but as we all know, diamonds aren't a boy's best friend, as my friend Marilyn Monroe keeps telling me. After just 4 weeks, John, at the age of 14 decided that perhaps bookbinding might be a better bet, and Bayntun's of Bath articled him for seven years apprenticeship. And so John was on his way. I'd loved to have been there when this shy boy joined the famous firm of bookbinders; George Bayntun's.

John took to bookbinding like he took to football; with graceful ease, and they put him into the finishing department, but he always had to be careful, otherwise he'd get a good burning by some of the cock-finishers. It taught John that to be a fine craftsman he would have to work hard and dedicate himself in order to become the best finisher that Bayntun's might ever have.

He was always restless and he decided to seek experience from other binderies in and around Bath, travelling mostly by pushbike. He was also very keen on the outdoors, a real adventurer. In the '50s his enthusiasm and keenness for the craft of bookbinding took him to Manchester and it was in Manchester he remained until he retired in the early '80s. I've met many of John's students who have said embarrassingly kind things about his teaching. He was so able to communicate the craft simply and with good humour.

John thought ahead and realised that bookbinding was no longer given the importance that it had once been. What could be done about it? He was always very single minded, he had spoken to his colleagues regarding his anxieties, and asked them all to meet him at the local pub to talk about what could be done. I know that there was much drinking done and they arranged to

John Coleman visits Paul in Chester.

meet the following week with ideas for the future of bookbinding. And so the Society of Bookbinders was formed in Manchester, and it was decided that John would be its natural leader.

It had to reach out to bookbinders, students and lovers of the old craft. It was felt that the Society would move ahead and have different areas around the country, and so the regions were born. I still think John's idea of the Society of Bookbinders and Book Restorers, as it was then known, was a brilliant idea. The first region of course was Manchester, then London, Bristol and Edinburgh, but then what? Do we know anybody in Wales who might start a region?

In the late 1970s I was living and working as a bookbinder in North Wales, bringing up a young family. I was binding away happily when the door bell rang. The dog and three small children ran to answer the door. It seems there were two gentlemen who had travelled from Manchester to visit me in my hidden corner of North Wales, John Coleman and Terry Walker.

"Children, let them in!"

After my wife refreshed them with a cool blend of Welsh tea, with tea-cakes and finely cut sandwiches, they told me the reason for their visit:

"Paul, we have started Societies all over the country and we are asking you to start one here in North Wales." said John hopefully.

"But John, I don't know anyone - I'm a small time bookbinder who works very much alone."

I was thrilled to be asked but what could I do? John and Terry decided on a different tack.

"Are there any good local pubs here, Paul?"

"Yes, there are a couple." I replied.

"Let's end our first stay in North Wales with a visit to one of them."

"Best idea so far!"

After a few glasses of wine, Welsh wine (which was tanned in Llandrindod Wells), I said;

"OK John, I shall gather you and Terry for our first ever meeting in Mold, the largest town nearby"

I had a slight worry - who do I invite? I know, I'll invite my friends Jill Scott and Geoff Brown. They have talents that I don't have. I invited a couple of farmers, a couple of doctors, three junior school teachers, a few friends and the usual hangers-on. Together we continued in our quest, or their quest, to start a region of the Society of Bookbinders.

"Paul, you have to have a committee. Jill, will you be the secretary? And Mr Brown, will you kindly be the treasurer?"

"John, what do I do?" I asked.

"Paul, you're the chairman."

"What do chairmen do?"

"The committee will rely on you for ideas and perhaps seek membership if you're lucky." he answered.

"John, I truly don't know anyone."

"Then look, let's blindly agree to a bookbinding programme"

And so we did. For the first time I realised using the Society's name had opened doors; the National Library of Wales in Aberystwyth being one of them. Many of the local bookshops and libraries would promote bookbinding and we would put on exhibitions. In a few months we had signed up 30 members and I was off to my first ever bookbinding conference in Manchester. The lone bookbinder was no longer, and it's all down to John Coleman and Terry Walker. John would go round the regions and show people the art of gold tooling, for me he was the best and most natural finisher I've ever known. But John's enthusiasm for teaching was also his greatest talent. As for myself, I could never be a good teacher, for I cannot explain myself. I have to lead by example. John could do both.

Ladies and gentlemen, we come to the end of this story and what am I left with? Nothing but envy. I really envied John for just one thing - that he could play football better than me. To be a boy international footballer - what a dream! That's it ladies and gentlemen, thank you for listening. Have a drink on John Coleman tonight, and make sure the wine isn't tanned in Wales. Thank you.

(A talk given by Paul C Delrue at the Education and Training Conference, University of Warwick, Friday 28th of August 2009.)

The Book of Jonah.
Thoughts and recollections by Paul C Delrue.
Foreword by the collector John R. Hodgson.

183

'Chester Play of the Deluge'

Paul Delrue first came to my notice in 1993 when I saw one of his bindings for sale at a book fair. Delightful though it was, I hadn't the courage to buy it and I went away empty handed. I regretted my decision and went back the next day to buy it. Thus was laid the foundation of my modest collection of fine bindings.

A subsequent visit to Paul's workshop (then in the heart of Chester) revealed to me the fascinating world of designer book-binding, and in 1994 I asked him to bind a copy of 'The Chester Play of the Deluge' (Rampant Lion Press, 1977). It seemed to be the perfect conjunction of binder and book; Paul was inspired by his association with Chester and by the engravings of David Jones, to produce one of his most beautiful bindings to date.

184

So delighted was I with the Deluge binding that, in 1996, I approached Paul with a view to his binding the sister book, 'The Book of Jonah'. This too was printed at the Rampant Lion Press and is also illustrated with David Jones' wonderful wood-engravings. It was a beautiful autumnal day when I met Paul at his new workshop in Tarvin.

'The Deluge' silk sewn headband.

When he saw the book, Paul responded with immediate enthusiasm and agreed to accept the commission. I left the design entirely to the binder, not wishing to inhibit his creativity, though I naturally hoped that the new binding would complement the existing one. I left Paul's workshop in a state of some excitement, tinged with a slight feeling of anxiety; would Paul really enjoy the commission, or had he perhaps taken it on more-or-less reluctantly, and how could the new binding possibly live up to the achievement of its predecessor? One of the thrills of commissioning a work is that you never quite know what you are going to get. Paul now continues the story:

Giving 'The Deluge' a good polish: A silk like finish.

DAY1: *Friday 27th December, 1996.*

What's on Radio 3? Music to suit without being bullied first thing in the morning. 'The Book of Jonah' was kindly given to me as a commission by John Hodgson during the late summer but I always felt it was really a winter binding. A nice size book with rather dense, black wood engravings by David Jones; 13 in all. It was the attractive pale green titling that I admired. It was so right, and from the very start Jonah was certainly going to be very fishy. Green and wavy in my new-style; 'painting with leather' (not 'colour by numbers'). I bind according to my day-to day feelings (a risky business), but it's a method I am used to and at ease with.

The book is rather easy to pull; I was surprised it only had three sections, rather heavy mould-made paper. My Jonah is number 103 out of a numbered edition of 300. As always with the start of a design I feel nervous and edgy, it always seems like a first performance. I must play some of Bax's sea music to put me in the mood. I feel all over the place - good coffee beckons.

Just before Christmas I hurried and finished a fine binding as a Christmas present – 'Sonnets of Dark Love' by Federico Garcia Lorca. Much has been taken out of me as nervous energy – it's very difficult to start again but I must. I always find leading in end - papers difficult, but an important first step. I must have looked at hundreds of sheets - a long haul.

DAY 3: *Sunday 29th December, 1996.*

I like working on Sundays. The weather is bright, crisp and very cold. I love binding when it's cosy and warm inside, the perfect time for boarding up. The lightweight boards (dark millboard) will be held to the book by a hinging strip of linen on both the inside and the outside. I prefer slightly larger squares than do most design bookbinders. Also, as the bottom edge and fore edge were left deckled, I must be very careful when cutting squares for these.

Exposed sewing? It's not for me! I much prefer the 'exposed' hidden - for safety reasons. The less seen, the better. Back to squares - leave a little air when attaching the boards, this allows room for the leather to go over the spine - a little give for a more comfortable opening.

While working I listen to Radio 3 or 4. The radio is a great friend. Radio 3 relaxes me in the mornings and the joy of music and bookbinding blend quite beautifully. A good play in the afternoon can be enjoyable too. Sometimes I wake in the morning and listen to sounds (without the radio). My mind is fresh and alert - just peace, and quiet recollections. Mornings really are the best time of the day.

After lining with linen, both sides of each board are lined with Kraft paper applied with a paste/PVA mixture and left to dry out before being put into the nipping press overnight. Remember to insert water proof card inside the boards before pressing.

187

DAY 4: *Monday 30th December, 1996*

On taking them out of the nipping press, I find that the boards work well but the book itself is a little tight. All in all though, it seems to handle comfortably. Andrew Brown, my assistant, is spending time looking for the colours of the sea in my very large box of leather. I am quite picky but he is very patient and keeps looking. I've pared a leather strip, covered the spine and set the headcaps. I can now start to apply wavy forms in leather straight onto the boards. The art form begins... All the ideas are in me. I have looked again and again at the illustrations and have a general idea of what I'm looking for. So what have I got? Colour, texture, slightly pictorial images and a head full of ideas.

I will start with a slightly uneven sky, dark blue etc. Before any work is carried out I make up a protective paper cap to keep the text block clean while working. I have also sandpapered the leather spine strip before working directly on the spine and boards. First to be applied is a piece of dark green. Off we go...

DAY 5: *Tuesday 31st December, 1996.*

Put down the first leather pieces onto the boards - quite large, difficult to pare and quite horny, dried-up old skin. Very grainy, dark green - beautiful when sanded. Lots of marine shapes, strong and watery. The skin is about one hundred years old I would have thought. I've worked the whole of the boards with it, about 30 pieces in all. The sanding is truly most frustrating; hot and dirty and I shall spend hours at it. Surely that's what craftsmanship is all about; it should be rewarding! I now add colour - more dark shades of green. Tomorrow is New Years Day and a good time to work uninterrupted. I will be able to gather my thoughts while paring and sanding.

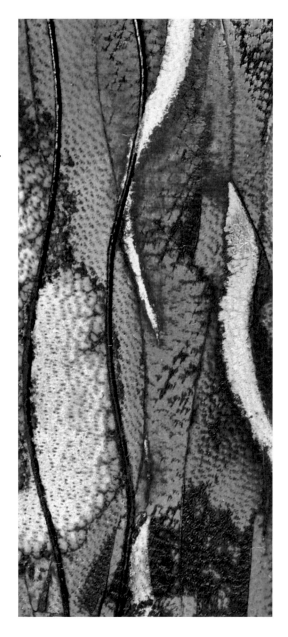

188

(After a period of ill-health it was nice to get back to work and feel the reassurance of the leather. I had faced returning to

Jonah with some apprehension but soon felt more relaxed as the book took me over again.)

A seagull in flight.

189

DAY 6: *Friday 7th February, 1997.*

This is a most difficult binding to return to. I have built up a number of layers and onlayed a rust coloured leather on top of my all-over green onlays. The rust coloured onlays present an outline of a sea-worthy boat together with puckered sails etc. The puckering is heavy as I will be covering it all over in wavy strips of green which, when sanded, will make waves (a stormy picture). I must work slowly but surely. The idea is still in my head, (dangerous thing these days!). I am growing excited as the ideas seem to begin to work. I normally work directly onto the boards and, hopefully, a picture emerges.

DAY 7: *Saturday 8th February, 1997.*

Worked nine hours today. The leather is building up and shows promise.

DAY 8: _Sunday 9th February, 1997._

Started at 9.00 this morning. Still paring for hours (dark greens) and then cutting the leather into wavy strips. I must have applied at least 100 strips so far. Sunday is a day for Jazz and thinking. Nipping to the village shop for The Sunday Times (a quick read through from the back) and then tea and Corn-Flakes. It's funny, I rarely get telephone calls on Sunday mornings; people must still be in bed! I must work in fits and starts so as not to over tire myself. I feel very happy to be working - left off at 7.30 in the evening.

DAY 9: _Monday 10th February, 1997._

At last I have completed the onlays of grey skies with plenty of pucker. The skies will be stormy and suit the weathered seas. The sandpapering begins tomorrow so the effect will be seen better. I have worked 8 hours on the sky!

190

DAY 10: _Tuesday 11th February, 1997._

Now for medium grade sandpaper all over the covers and then watery PVA. It takes about 10 applications. The sanding is done by hand, finishing off with a fine paper almost as a polish. The different textured leathers are showing to interesting effect. I wonder how it will look towards the end?

DAY 11: _Saturday 15th February, 1997._

Today is my son's 21st birthday. Had a quick telephone chat with him. We will eat out with his friends and drink his health in the late evening at The Boot Inn in Willington, an adjacent village. I'm quite happy to sand and apply watery PVA during the day. I have decided to add a little more colour for effect. The feel and atmosphere of the cover is ideal but it lacks impact. The sanding continues until I feel the emerging shapes bring interest and pleasure. Minimalist bindings seem to be the in-thing these days - but not for me! I like my bindings, if possible, to mystify and add a little wonder. Why did he do it like that? Does it work? Is it showing off too much? More and more craft today appears riddled with artwork which can look over-dressed. Then there can be a dullness, when binders put on as little as possible. Sometimes there's binding by technique; again, not for me! I'm not fond of lumps and bumps. My books must feel right (like silk) and create atmosphere; a painter's eye perhaps.

I have added birds and more 'sea' but it needs a little more storm so the impact is darker and more dense; the feeling of hopelessness and of losing.

DAY 12: *Sunday 16th February, 1997.*

Marcel's birthday was a splendid affair with plenty of good food and a very fine wine - Australian, highly recommended.

The weather today is good for bookbinding – it's dull and overcast, and the church bells of St Andrew's ring loud and clear, a lovely Sunday noise, such a refined sound. I think the 'The Book of Jonah' is coming on well with the light, bird-like overlays giving a link between the back and front covers. The binding must be understated, giving only a hint of what I'm getting at. It could be finished this week although there is still more sanding and watery PVA to come.

DAY 13: *Monday 17th February, 1997.*

I have written to John Hodgson inviting him to visit and see the book as it is now taking shape. I'm still adding leather, sanding and PVAing. It is still not wholly working but I hope that this week with see it through to the bitter end. Perhaps I will put in some blind tooling in a wavy formation. The book lacks something, I'm not sure what. Still, I'm hopeful that John will like it. My mind also works toward the inside; I have many ideas floating about. For the first time I have worked in the evening again, sanding, applying the watery PVA and adding 'fishy' leathers. I'm nearly there, I think.

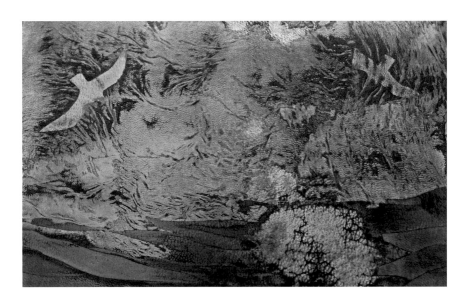

DAY 14: _Thursday 20th February, 1997._

My wandering, wavy lines are giving the picture a 'together' look. At last it's working! It has a three-dimensional appearance and the latest colour is a welcome contrast to the darker greens. From the start I had never seen the water as blue, more as green. The illustrations were a little dense but my design was always going to be a suggestion of the inside. It's worked out a little more pictorial than I first thought and, as such, has created much movement and interest.

I am feeling so much better today; my mind is comfortable, ready and clear. I'm still sanding and PVAing, 4 coats today. After medium sandpaper I revert to fine sanding to give it a smooth and silky finish and it begins to handle well. I like my books to be handled and touched without white gloves.

DAY 15: _Saturday 1st March, 1997._

I have left Jonah in the press - a very light pressing, to rest and settle. I have put a dark green leather joint inside and have found, as always, that the book closes with great difficulty, so a rest is needed.

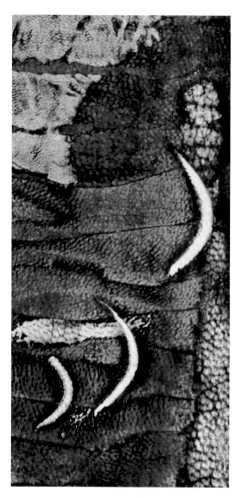

Today I will put in a filler after trimming out the leather turn-ins and joint. My turn-ins will measure one quarter of an inch, really quite narrow. After 24 hours I will line the filler with archival Kraft paper and sand it level all round.

The boards will be comfortable and even and, more importantly, will be part of the book. I am still thinking of colour when I'm working; what will match and what will pull the binding together? A comfortable partnership between the outside and the inside. The binding is once again becoming exciting.

N.B. The filler is put down with a mixture of PVA and paste but mostly PVA. The Kraft paper is put down 24 hours later with just PVA. I must make sure that the boards do not pull in too much when the final leather is put down inside.

DAY 16: _Sunday 2nd March, 1997._

A beautiful Sunday; warm sunlight coming into the bindery and the distant church bell ringing. What more could one want?

Today is doublures day. The Irish green leather matches the lettering on the title page beautifully. To get the right feeling it is important to match the colour as you enter the first few pages of the book.

The leather of the doublures went down nicely onto a matching bright green flyleaf. The suede was edge-pared and tipped against the leather joint. After a couple of hours, it was neatly brought down onto the pasted fly-leaf. It was then rubbed down before being lightly pressed.

DAY 17: _Tuesday 4th March, 1997._

Missed an appointment at the hospital; total forgetfulness, telephone to apologise and arrange another appointment (feel bad about it, though). At last I've dared to add blind tooling on the front board. The boat was drawn roughly on paper first and then the impression was pressed through with a sharp bone folder. The drawing was positioned around the reddish shapes on the front cover. After blind tooling through the paper template, it was removed and the impressions were tooled again to achieve a clearer line before being inked in. It looks quite good. I sanded again to get a clearer picture. I put the book into the press but just very lightly.

DAY 18: _Wednesday 5th March, 1997._

A bright day. Pared the emerald green leather for doublures. I have left the leather a little bigger all around to allow for a little puckering (half inch). I also continued blind tooling on the outside covers at the base of the boards. The wavy lines were blinded in, free-hand on the front and back covers, these lines will continue onto the doublures inside.

It's now working like a dream, matching the title page beautifully. I've managed to complete the doublures, putting them down with a paste/PVA mix to avoid them pulling the boards in too much. The balance is all-important. I then start to work on the finish; the puckered leather is sanded with a very fine glasspaper to remove the bright look and then I continue my very free wavy lines from the outside covers onto the doublures. The lines off-set nicely onto the suede flyleaves when the book is closed.

The final finish.

195 It's now looking more or less complete but I feel that I must add smaller light blue onlays to give a distant effect of tranquillity; to reduce the stormy look. The book continues to handle well and feels comfortable.

DAY 19: *Saturday 15th March, 1997.*

The last part is the box, which will be a simple protective up-and-over box in green waterproof buckram, lined in dark green suede. The box will also have the blind wavy lines at head and tail and the full title on the spine. At this stage I'm not sure whether to title in black or in gold or to apply a decorative label with gold lettering.

It's a beautiful day, bright and sunny. I will write to John Hodgson telling him his Jonah is ready for collection. I wonder what he will think.

DAY 20: *Sunday 10th March, 1997.*

I am still working on the design by sanding and applying

diluted PVA. It still needs honing and refining until I'm satisfied that it has the beauty of a painter's touch, but I feel close to being at ease with it.

DAY 21: _Tuesday 11th March, 1997._

A beautiful day; the garden full of daffodils. Today I have finished the box, simply titled in gold on the spine.

At last I have completed 'The Book of Jonah'. It has become an old friend over the last four months and I feel a little strange now that my work is over. This binding has held me together during a period when I have had to contemplate the possibility of not being able to work following my illness.

DAY 22: _Wednesday 12th March, 1997._

I am now lightly sanding all over the covers, opening the leaves and making sure that the book fits snugly into the box. The suede flyleaves and the suede inside the box are given a final brushing and cleaning.

I phone John and invite him to come to Tarvin; the book is ready. We have agreed on the 24th of March. It means the book can rest. All books should rest. I am not sure how many hours I have worked on the book but I suppose it would be about a 100 hours - happy hours. I am now trying to reflect on this, my latest work. Will it stand the test of time? Will it fully represent me? Do I feel at my bookbinding best? I have always said my best years would be between 50 and 65. I am 53 in July. Is this, then, the best of me?

John calls tomorrow morning for 'The Book of Jonah'. I will hand it over at 10 o'clock. It has worked well and I am truly happy with it. My friends like it - although some, like me, had their usual doubts until the book was completed.

I work on ideas and build one upon another until I know

how it will work out. It's always difficult to see the finish but the end result has to please; warm and soft to the touch. A picture to capture the imagination. A mixture of textures all gathering together until it mirrors my thoughts. This binding is a turning point; my life is fuller for its completion. How fortunate I am to be able to spend so many pleasurable hours doing the things I simply love to do.

The collector's response:

My fears over the commission were entirely unfounded. The new binding is simply awe-inspiring. There is a wonderful sense of motion in the wave shapes and the bird-like figures which roll and sweep both vertically and horizontally across the covers, reflecting the dynamism of David Jones' engraving. One also feels that the technique of applying layer upon layer of leather onlays imparts to the binding a depth which mirrors the multiple planes of the illustrations.

'The Book of Jonah' has a more representational binding than 'The Deluge'. It is smaller, more detailed and intimate, which is perhaps appropriate to its subject matter (the story of one man's odyssey, as opposed to the sin of humanity and global cataclysm). Seagulls plunge through leaden skies on both covers, while on the front cover, picked out in blind tooling, are the hapless vessel and the whale that swallowed Jonah.

A too-literal representation of the story has wisely been avoided. The blind-tooled waves running across both covers and doublures act as a unifying motif. The doublures of sanded green leather are perhaps inspired by Will Carter's magnificent double title-page printed in green and black - the tonal match is perfect yet they are almost vegetal in both colour and texture, calling to mind seaweed or the gourd which grew to provide shade for Jonah. The colour theme is also continued in the drop-back box which likewise carries the blind tooled waves.

As a postscript I should like to add that, until I read Paul's diary, I hadn't fully appreciated how much effort, both physical and emotional, the binder puts into his or her work. It is sobering to realise that my commission caused Paul such anxiety, but satisfying that it was ultimately so rewarding. My admiration of the binding is greatly enhanced. However, I believe that the feeling of an owner (or, as I see myself, a temporary custodian) towards a binding can rarely match the emotional intensity of its creator (who has invested so much more) and that, in the end, Jonah is more Paul's book than mine.

J.R.H.

John Handley, a Commission:
The client's perspective on Paul Delrue's binding of 'Hannibal'.

It was in December 1996 that I decided to visit Paul Delrue in his bindery at Tarvin, near Chester. In moving from Chester to Tarvin in June of that year he had found the peace and quiet that had previously proved so elusive. This change in Paul's location was having a profound influence on the way he was able to approach his work. There were fewer interruptions and he was able to give more time for reflection on what he was doing. I had known Paul for several years and was an admirer of his work, particularly the imaginative and often innovative way he handled his 'pictures in leather', but it had taken me a long time to pluck up the courage to commission a fine binding. This account tries to give the client's perspective and attempts to explain how Paul is developing his new direction and technique.

The book I had chosen for the Delrue treatment was Sir Gavin De Beer's 'Hannibal', with 232 plates, sixteen of which were in colour. Originally published in 1969, I had purchased the first reprint in 1974 and it had been on my shelf since then. It was an unusually challenging theme, enlarging upon the great struggle for power in the Mediterranean between Carthage and Rome.

My interest began well over thirty years ago when I had listened to a radio programme that described an adventurous journey made in a Dormobile from New Cartagena in Spain across the Pyrenees, along the southern French coast, up the Rhone Valley and then, taking what was a historically controversial route based on the researches of the classical scholar Sir Gavin De Beer, over the Alps into northern Italy. De Beer had devoted a lifetime's study to the literary, archaeological and scientific evidence relating to Hannibal and his historical background.

On the basis of his considerable research into the changes affecting climate, terrain, river flows and the territories of the various transalpine tribes of Gaul, he had put forward new and convincing arguments to support his theory for the route taken by Hannibal. It was in 218 BC, into the plain of Piedmont near the source of the river Po that, like a clap of thunder, Hannibal burst out of the Alps to descend upon the unsuspecting Romans. Fascinated by the story of how Hannibal, intent upon revenge, had defeated one Roman army after another and defied his enemies for over fifteen years I just knew I had to read more about this

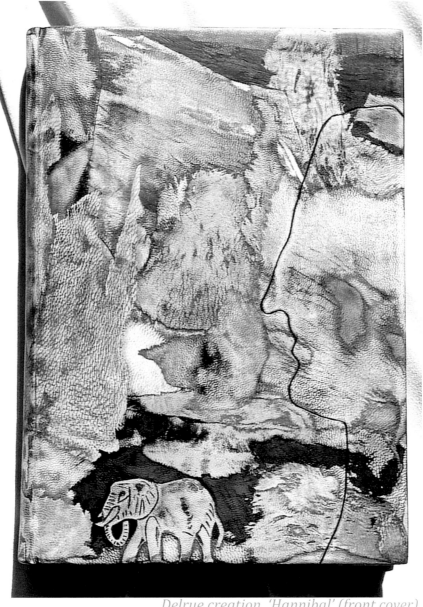

200

Delrue creation, 'Hannibal' (front cover).

remarkable man. Years later when I started to do some very amateurish binding of my own and met Paul Delrue, I knew that one day I would want Paul to do a special leather binding which I felt would present him with a striking challenge, and at the back of my mind I knew that it would be my favourite book on Hannibal.

<u>*Background.*</u>

How would Paul deal with the task of a leather binding for a book that had such great themes of adventure, heroism, revenge and tragedy? I think it is fair to say that until now most of Paul's bindings reflected literary or artistic themes, so an historic story packed with action and adventure would be something new. Paul is not fond of travelling and, not surprisingly, he had never been to the French Alps. He asked me to leave him photographs of my visits to the French Alps in 1966 and 1993.

201

The pictures I left with Paul included the tortuous Gorge des Gaz, where Hannibal's army was attacked from the heights above by one of the mountain tribes, and the pass of the Col de

Grimone where Hannibal won his first battle of the Alps. I also left pictures of the rock in the valley of Queyras, thought to have been where Hannibal had one of his camps, and the pass which was favoured by De Beer and others as a possible crossing point into Italy, the Col de La Traversette, which is over 9500 feet high. In addition I loaned Paul a copy of the popular writings of Livy, who had a reluctant admiration for Rome's enemy and also the lavishly illustrated book Hannibal's Footsteps by Bernard Levin. I knew that Paul wanted to absorb all that he could about Hannibal and his astonishing decision to attack across the fearsome Alps and take the Romans by surprise.

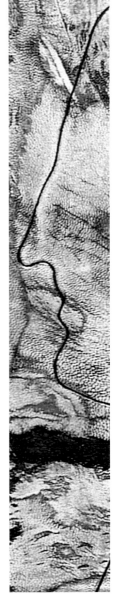

It was always my intention to leave Paul to work on the project in his own time. It was not something to be hurried. Nevertheless, I gave him a call on 11 April to see how things were going. It was then that I discovered that Paul had suffered a minor stroke on New Year's Day which had affected his left arm and hand. Paul was worried about the effect upon his work, and the project was on hold; I reassured him that there was no hurry. Paul warned me that once he got started he would work quickly and that I was to come promptly when his call came if I wished to see the progress of the binding before completion. The call came on 26 June but by the time I was able to visit four days later the main binding was complete.

I was astonished, the effect was quite dazzling: it was like peering into the past. It was as though the mist had cleared and there were the blues and greys of a great mountainous terrain, overlooked by the hawkish outline of the great Carthaginian general. Two African elephants were also represented but they

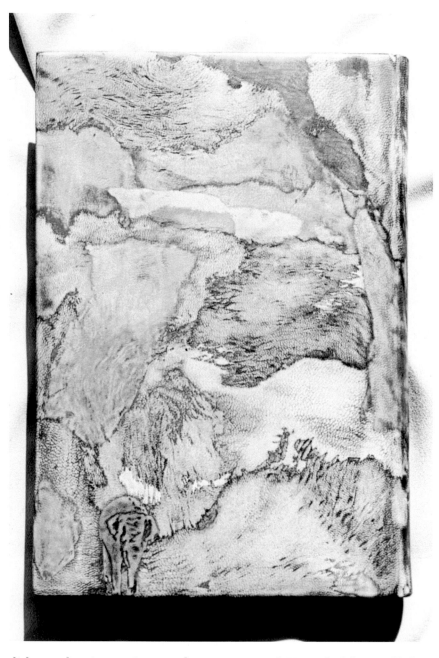

did not dominate; it was the terrain and Hannibal himself that caught the eye. The three-dimensional effect of the leather binding meant that you tended to see a different outline as you continued looking. How had Paul achieved this very satisfying effect?

Hannibal takes over.

Although Paul is a very instinctive binder, you would be quite mistaken to think that he develops his design concept as he goes along. His thoughts about Hannibal began months earlier, not only concerning colours and the general shape of the design, but also the way the book was to be worked; just as much thought was

Refining Hannibal.

given to the forwarding as to the design and finish. At the start Paul can feel nervous and edgy rather like an artist about to start a performance. A great deal of preparatory thought went into the selection of decorative fly-leaves and the type, colour and texture of the end-papers, as Paul knows that they form the heart of his design and determine the outcome of the emerging colours on the covers.

He began by pulling the book, and the thick sections of art paper were re-sewn on five tapes, each 12mm wide, and the hand-decorated endpapers were sewn on as a normal section. The spine was glued up with a thin coating of PVA and, after making sure that all was square, the text-block was lightly pressed overnight. The next morning the book was rounded and backed and, in turn, the edges were trimmed by press and plough, preparatory to edge colouring. Each edge was lightly sanded and a size of watery paste was applied as a base for the colouring with acrylics: The aim was to give an overall blue effect with hints of grey and green. After the ten minutes drying time for the final edge, the book was removed from the laying press with the usual sense of relief that the edge colouring has worked. Double silk headbands in pale blue and green were sewn, and the spine was lined with Irish linen and a hollow back of archival kraft paper. Paul was now ready to attach the boards. In the interests of flexibility, strength and, ultimately, shape, the boards were made up of laminate layers of millboard and archival paper. The text-block was attached by lacing the tapes into the boards and the book was then put into the press overnight. After sandpapering the boards Paul was ready to start putting on a protective quarter of leather down the spine, and a strip of leather around the head, fore edge, and tail edges of the boards.

From the start, Paul had had an overall idea of the colours and shape of the design, but once work was underway, the choice and arrangement of colours changed as the work progressed; much to Paul's own surprise, and as he himself said, the book "just seemed to take over." The final process began by laying on the boards quite large pieces of Harmatan goatskin leather which had been pared and the edges bevelled: These were applied so that the pieces of leather overlapped each other, and occasionally the pieces were cut to suitably random shapes. To describe the process as a 'collage' is not quite accurate, because Paul is striving for a pictorial impression, whereas a collage arranges unrelated materials. He looks for what he describes as, "pieces with interesting marks or lines, often the harder parts of the animal's skin." They are pieces which others might consider, at a superficial glance, as unattractive or even blemished.

At this stage his head was full of ideas: Hannibal had set out on his great adventure across the Alps with thirty-seven elephants, and this association would be what people would expect to see, but Paul was only too aware that he must not allow the elephants to dominate the binding. After giving the matter a great deal of thought, Paul decided that the emphasis had to be on Hannibal and the importance of his achievement.

Paul visualised the book in mainly blue and grey. The reason lay in the Alpine terrain, in the pictures studied by Paul and in the history of the subject. According to Livy, Hannibal began his ascent of the Alps in the 'season of the setting of the Pleiades', in October. As they approached, Hannibal's men saw the towering peaks, the snow-clad pinnacles soaring to the sky. All nature, we are told, was stiff with frost, but it did not begin to snow until the army had reached the summit of the pass into Italy.

Paul spent the next two days applying more overlapping greys, with particular interest in those pieces having a 'blue-ish' tinge, with small pieces of white and light greens. The 'lacunose process' involves sanding down the pieces of leather with medium grade sandpaper after a very watery PVA solution has been applied. When the leather is dry enough to feel slightly tacky, sanding commences. The sanded leather looks and feels beautiful. It is warm work, with Paul sanding down by hand at least twenty times. The paring is time consuming and sometimes the leather has to be cut into appropriate shapes. While the pieces are still moveable Paul likes to make some of the onlays with a pushing or squeezing motion which 'rucks' or 'puckers' the leather into fine ridges. The sanding smoothes out these ridges leaving a fine almost polished finish to the touch, but now the former ridges appear as naturally jagged fissure lines in the alpine rock face. Further sanding using medium grade paper can create holes or gaps as part of one leather piece reveals another colour from a previous layer underneath in what I call 'the lacunose effect'.

At this stage Paul felt that the book, which measures 23.8 by 16.5 cm, was going almost too well.

"I was amazed", commented Paul, "at how quickly the book seemed to take shape."

As Paul had arranged the pieces, examining the flesh side

of each piece of leather for colour and texture, he had felt the need to create landscape height. The landscape should not appear gentle: Pictures of Mount Viso encircled in cloud showed that an ominous impression had to be created. At last, Paul was looking less and less at the illustrations and the leather was taking over and, bearing in mind the vastness of the canvas being created, he decided to place a small, simplified outline of an elephant on the front board and on the back board of the book.

The last act.

The final touch which Paul bestowed on my book was a daring one. It was the product of much thought: An outline of Hannibal on the front board. There are no known pictures of the great man but there is a beardless head of Melqart on the reverse of a silver double shekel struck at Carthage c.220 BC which is generally regarded as a portrait of Hannibal. He looks a commanding figure, with a straight nose, a strong forehead and an open expression with, perhaps, a certain travel weariness. Paul drew the outline on paper and made an impression of the outline on the covered board with a pointed, but not sharp, bone folder. On removing the paper he creased further into the leather

Paul and John Handley discuss 'Hannibal' at the Tarvin Bindery.

and used a Hi-Tec V5 extra fine pen to ink in the form. It worked beautifully.

Paul decided not to use suede on the inside of the boards and instead completed with reversed leather flyleaves, with matching doublures of light, veined grey. While the finishing touches were being added Paul made his usual practical 'up and over' protective box, covered in grey Arbelave Buckram and lined with soft grey suede, with the title in black on the box spine.

A few simple mountains in black outline were added on the front. The book received a final watery PVA sanding down as Paul continued to hone and refine his creation, continually searching for that polished silky feel and look, rather like a painter's final touch. Paul likes his bindings to have an air of mystery about them. There is never too much art work or technical brilliance to distract. In fact, Paul has said that he likes the binding to be understated. In this respect, I think he has succeeded brilliantly with Hannibal, for there is a picture to capture the imagination.

For my part I have a binding that is beautiful to behold, with a patina that is lovely to handle and, equally important, a binding that can be opened and read comfortably. Perhaps I was more fortunate than I realised in waiting all those years before commissioning Paul. If I had done so a few years earlier, Paul believes that I would have got a more literal, pictorial representation, whereas he feels now that he has at last found his way. This is a style which displays greater maturity firmly based on a lifetime's experience: His 'lacunose' and stratified style of impressionistic leather binding has come of age.

It's Quite Beautiful, but why so Depressing?
My Final Speech.

The hall was packed to hear my final speech, I was to talk about my life story as a bookbinder, but how was I to hold the audience for an hour or so? Some had travelled many miles to hear my final words. The bookbinding world, family and friends, they all turned up (an unfriendly crowd) to hear me make a poor show, to give a little of myself away, to fall off to sleep as soon as the lights were dimmed. I was old and tired, but I did not want to let the people from another world down.

I had been planning my speech for many months. It never works on the page, it doesn't feel honest and right. I had to look at the audience and count the empty seats, but there were none. It was busy and full with many standing. Why me, why did they want to hear me? They all knew I had just written a book, a book about my life story, my memories, mostly of dead faces.

I was quite a good bookbinder. It gave me the greatest pleasure and it was all down to luck, to have been given magical hands, to put mind to fingers; the delight of hours with lonesome thoughts, planning ideas to put into my bindings. But, did I have the skill? I was always afraid that someday I would lose my gift and I always worked feeling insecure. I've always had to fight my nature. It has been a lifetime battle with myself. I never bind for anyone but myself, it always hinged on this boy from the home. They, along with the Sisters were willing me on, the boys were smiling with fear on their faces but I had to hold the audience. Introductions were made but I could not live up to what was said. It was all too good and untrue. The lights in the large hall were on me, all I felt was uneasy anticipation. I closed my eyes for a second then I opened them to hear generous and warm applause, it seemed to go on and on. I just stood and smiled as I looked into the dark.

"Thank you all for coming." I said slowly as I took my reading notes out of my jacket pocket.

I hesitated. I did not want to talk to the night's faceless features. I had dropped my reading glasses and was sitting awkwardly. I mumbled a few words, but nothing came out. I walked down the steps slowly and was shaking with fear. I could hear whispers and talking:

"What's wrong with him, I expect it's nerves and he's all in, looks a sad mess."

At last, I opened my mouth agreeing that they were right to honour me with words of encouragement, they were right to hear me speak of bookbinding and understand perhaps. You see, I am a human being, I can no longer live with myself. I have nothing more to give, to be truthful, all my life I have tried to do my level best to give freely the knowledge of a man who has been binding books for years. All the Delrue answers are in the book, and I can tell you its title at last, it's called 'My Soul has no Friends'. How do you spend your life with people who no longer care? I simply wanted to be loved but love will have to be reinvented, it died many years ago.

I am left with beautiful images. I long to walk in the green fields of Wales, with him, reading poetry. I'm better, deeply better to have known the beauty of love, that's all that matters. But I owe you more perhaps than the truth of words. Shouting, a voice in the very back row said;

"What about your inventions, Lacunose and your Tudor Styles, your paintings with leather, and perhaps knowing you have added to the work of bookbinding?"

I had been given compliments, perhaps unknowingly. My work was summed up like this: It is all very clever drawing pretty pictures on books, but how much better they are on canvas. I answered that all I wished was to bind the beautiful ideas I could only dream about, but you know ladies and gentlemen I have never been to art college, my art is undisciplined and to make matters worse I do not have a style. My bindings are all in my head, the excitement of carrying them over onto a book cover is some kind of magic. I can never be a paper design planner. To get the best out of me I have to bind from my feelings, for I have never studied art or colour or how to hold a brush. What I see and feel is all I have to give, nothing else matters. I can only marvel at other bookbinders who can offer some kind of guideline. I cannot, it simply comes, even as an apprentice;

"Sir, let me get on with it."

Exhibition at my Bindery (Ruthin).

I went my own way, I never planned a thing, how could I? I even tried to explain myself once but failed miserably. I just close my eyes and let it pour out. I see it all in colour first, then images to suit the book and then the most important part; carrying out the work. I always have to be alone. I need my own space to watch the binding grow, to become part of me, it's that simple I promise. But, before I finish, let me tell you all a true story from Wales, it happened like this:

Two old ladies visited me in my Ruthin Bindery Exhibition. I had on exhibition samples of fine leather bindings. My leather pictures, photograph albums full of my work, sketch books, poetry and my own history of bookbinding. I wanted to sell to the public the real beauty of binding. My apprentice and I left the old ladies to handle the design bindings, many that I had bound as a teenager, lots of decorative marbled papers, there was so much to touch and see. My pictures in leather were of great interest, after all, my pictures were original and very unlike traditional

'Write as short as you can, In order, of what matters.'

bindings of which there were many, displayed on the open shelves. After the ladies had spent a couple of hours they waved me over to thank me and showed their admiration of my work.

"It is quite beautiful, but why so depressing?"

They were the last words they said to me when leaving the Bindery. Why so depressing? My work had affected them, I had at last won the battle, I was able to move the two old ladies. My work at last reached heights I hardly expected. It felt like a part of me watching my own death, watching; turn over stones and watch life's secrets scatter. The red hill full of living blood, fly at night. Perhaps it was my writings and pictures that made them depressed.

Ladies and Gentlemen I cannot do happiness and joy. I can only fight and keep on hurting in the battle with myself. I will leave you with something that has been said of me through these many years. Look into his eyes, they seem always to have suffered, such painful eyes, perhaps he has secrets that he wishes us not to know, perhaps he walks without a shadow. The large audience left the hall quietly, the lights were turned off and I was left alone, sharing my footsteps with no other. I left the hall at peace and not hanging onto anyone's words. I had nothing more to say, but, thank you.

212

The Folding Star. *By Alan Hollinghurst.*

'The Folding Star', Booker binding 1995.

The events of 'The Folding Star' are played out amongst the silent streets and canals of a city that seems locked in the past, and across the northern landscape of out-of-season resorts and abandoned houses that lie beyond. The school teacher, Edward, is introduced to the world of the enigmatic and reclusive Symbolist painter, Orst, who took his own life during the Nazi occupation.

It is a story whose central enigma is unresolved until its very last lines. I have been deeply affected by this beautiful, poetically-written novel.

'The Folding Star' by Alan Hollinghurst.
Chatto & Windus, London, 1994 (Booker binding).
Bound in the Lacunose style, 1995.

Un Nos Ola Leuad (One Moonlit Night).
By Caradog Prichard.

'*One Moonlit Night*' is Delrue's first binding of a Welsh text. This marvellous book, which is a rich blend of deep dark blacks, greys and ocean blues is unashamedly pictorial. The journey of the unhappy boy begins on the front cover, with the Welsh slate houses and ends on the doublure (inside back cover) as the boy drowns in a fiery sea. I think it's a perfectly realised gem of a binding - tasteful, heartbreaking and gloomy.

It was sold recently in America to a South African: It 's a Welsh literary masterpiece, bound by an Englishman with a French name, travelling through America on its way to Johannesburg! It is written in a deceptively simple, lyrical style, but can be read on several levels.

'Un Nos Ola Leuad' (inside cover).

Narrated in the first person, it starts out as a boys exuberant view of his world, unwittingly, against a backdrop of appalling deprivation during the First World War. As the boy, with his friends Huw and Moi, comes of age, the assumed sanity and surety of their world begins to fall apart and the story builds to an excruciating climax, as shocking as it is profound. This moving work is one of the most powerful Welsh language novels to be published since the Second World War.

'Un Nos Ola Leuad' by Caradog Prichard.
Printed by Gwasg Gee, Denbigh 1953.
Bound in the Lacunose style, 1997.

Romeo and Juliet. *By William Shakespeare.*

Miniature binding for Neale M Albert, bound by Paul Delrue in Llandudno, North Wales, New Year 2005, in honour of the bard. A Tudor binding. A theatrical treat with many colours of goatskin leather in tan, purple, lilac, blossom, yellow, rust, blue and grey with figures of our young couple onlayed in natural on the front cover with blind decoration outlining 'Romeo and Juliet'. The book has been French sewn by Andrew Brown, with coloured endpapers, suede fly leaves and colourful leather doublures matching the covers of the miniature binding. It's miniature binding number five, not many since I started as an apprentice in 1959. You either love them or find them too fiddly; it is still a fight to work small. I trimmed by press and plough and hand coloured the edges using acrylics, again matching my colourful design on the covers. Complete with protective up and over box, covered with book cloth and lined inside with suede.

I treated Shakespeare as theatre, as a performance, as colour. We all know the story of 'Romeo and Juliet', for never was a story more woe than this of Juliet and her Romeo.

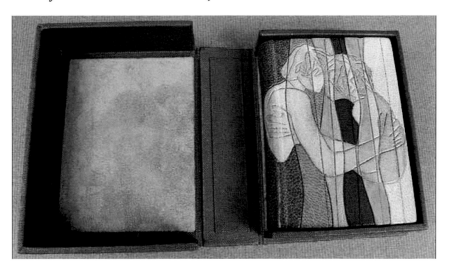

'Romeo and Juliet' by William Shakespeare.
Published by Knickerbocker Leather & Novelty Co, New York.
Bound in Llandudno, 2005.

The Flute of Sardonyx. By Edmund John.
Delrue Fine Binding. A Tender Binding.

The flute is worth more than a mere glance. The loss of boyhood, the inability any longer to recapture the passionate innocence of lost days:

> *'Dream days that lost themselves in your wide eyes,*
> *Where the dead longing of my own heart lies.'*

"*The Flute of Sardonyx*'

The flute was, not surprising then, John's first major publication. He died in 1917 at the early age of thirty four, almost certainly by his own hand.

Binding: 'Harmatan' goatskin various shades of material (light biscuit colours), outline of a boy's face in onlayed dark red. My tudor style. I was very much influenced by the beautiful images by Nicholas Wilde.

This collection of poems first appeared in 1913 but has fallen, perhaps understandably but undeservedly, into oblivion. Edmund John's poetry has a sensuous beauty and the authentic voice of love and loss. Following what was almost a fashion in the first two decades of the century, the objects of the emotion in many of the poems are boys but, unlike most of the Uranian poets, John's sincerity gives the poems a white hot purity.

It is this aspect of the text, together with intimations of the poet's agony at the loss of his own boyhood, that it is so hauntingly captured in Nicholas Wild's exquisite pencil drawings which are printed in the book by subtle lithography.

THE FLUTE OF SARDONYX

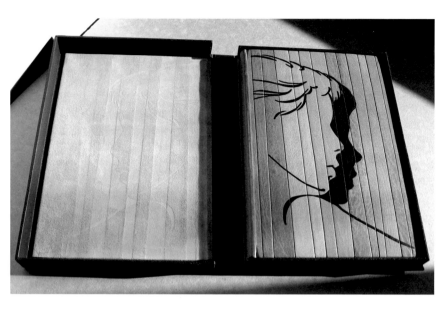

'The Flute of Sardonyx' in Spectrum type, Monotype set, with Centaur and Libra type handset. Printed on Rivoli paper using a FAG Control 900 press. Illustrated with 16 pencil drawings by Nicholas Wild which were litho printed by Adrian Lack of the Senecio Press. Only 260 copies were printed, all signed by the artist, this being 238. The Old Stile Press, Llandogo, Monmouthshire in the autumn of 1991. Private press.

'The Flute of Sardonyx' by Edmund John.
Printed at The Old Stile Press, Llandogo,
Monmouthshire 1991.
Bound in Llandudno, early springtime 2005.

Some years ago an elderly man almost fell into my bindery door. I helped him to a comfortable chair. From the inside pocket of his old jacket he produced a dirty brown envelope and asked me to open it carefully. Inside was a worn, discoloured cloth diary. By this time, Phillip, my apprentice had made him a cup of tea, which steadied him.

He sat with his head bowed and in a whisper told me how his brothers, like some 300,000 others, had died at The Battle of The Somme in

'The Unreturning' by Wilfred Owen.

220

northern France in 1916. They were aged just 16 and 17. This, the younger brother's diary, found in the mud of the Somme, was all he and his mother had by which to remember them - their bodies, like countless others, having never been identified.

The slim book was fragile and muddied but, incredibly, still intact. Difficult to open, it had never been fully read. I dared to look up and found him sitting upright with tears in his eyes - but not crying; that had been done long ago.

'The Unreturning'

A month later he came back to collect the repaired diary, saying he had found a museum willing to look after it. He had never married, spending his life looking after and comforting his mother into old age; a sad, lonely woman still crying over the loss of her two sons. Now he was able, for the first time, to read the words written in the diary and relive the weeks in 1916 when his brothers were both alive and had a future, and the stars were bright.

'The Somme: An Eyewitness History'

I didn't raise my son to be a soldier,
I brought him up to be my pride and joy.
Who dares to put a musket on his shoulder,
To kill some other mother's darling boy?

222

'Anthem for Doomed Youth' by Wilfred Owen.

Land. *Poems selected by Eric Williams.*

'Land' with Garrick Palmer illustrations.

223

Bound in the Tudor style. Mid-brown Harmatan goatskin with two Lacunose panels. Colours of azure blue skies, warm yellow cornfields and brown earth, with fences of black; perhaps

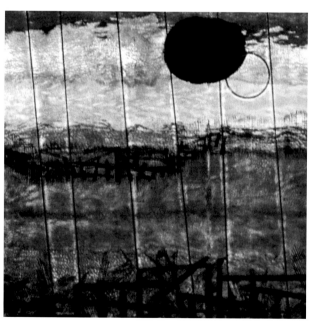

to keep people away from the farmers as they tend the land. I have added blind d e c o r a t i o n capturing my view and that of artist Garrick Palmer, who dominates this landscape book together with the beautifully chosen poems.

'Land', bound in 2007.

224

The titling is in black along the narrow spine in keeping with the feel of the book. "The design captures a warm sunny day - but perhaps with a chance of a little light wind to come as the days draw in."

Printed at The Old Stile Press, 1996.

Gone with the Wind. By Margaret Mitchell.

A fine Binding for Joshua Heller, Rare Books Inc. of Margaret Mitchell's 'Gone with the Wind'. It was bound in my new bindery 'Crispin,' Ruthin, North Wales, surrounded by beautiful hills for friends.

Gone with the Wind: New York, The Macmillan Company, May 1936. A 1st Edition. Set by Brown Brothers linotypers, printed in the United States of America by the Ferris Printing Company. An epic story of a lifetime made even more famous by the 1939 film which swept the boards at The Oscars. I have tried very hard to distance myself from that masterful, magnificent film; a favourite, a beautifully crafted film. When I was invited by Josh Heller to design bind this book I had no hesitation, a wonderful opportunity to re-read the book and capture my feelings on the book covers on a grand scale.

The binding uses a dark red goatskin from Harmatan of Northamptonshire. The book was sewn on five tapes, new

'Gone with the Wind'

endpapers, various colours, a light trim of the book edges ready for edge colouring using acrylics of strong colours. A battle scene perhaps, my colouring evokes atmosphere and intensity and it all leads onto the book covers. It is like looking through a large window, to fertile land growing for future generations. There are birds brooding above, waiting for the next chapter.

My binding had to be strong in colours but not illustrative, just a hint of the vast novel and it's characters. I have captured these colours on the inside boards. The leather onlays I have used white, rich yellow (trees) brown (fences) lacunose panels setting the scene. The binding is housed in a protective box, which has been covered in old fashioned rich yellow buckram, lined inside with suede. The title on the binding is old American style lettering onlay along the spine of the book. A book I have truly enjoyed binding.

Edge Decoration; 'wind on fire'.

The Music From Behind the Moon.
An Epitome by James Branch Cabell.

With eight wood engravings by Leon Underwood. Judge thou the lips of those that are rose against me and their devices against me all the day. Behold their sitting down, and their rising up:

"I am their music."

New York, The John Day Company, published September 1926 and printed in the United States of America. An edition limited to three thousand copies, printed by William Edward Rudge on Vidalon Velin paper, from the handset 'Garamond' type with typography by Byron J Musser. Bound by Paul C Delrue, Springtime 2009 and signed.

"Music is my life. If there be any music coming from behind the moon it echoes faintlier than does the crackle of the

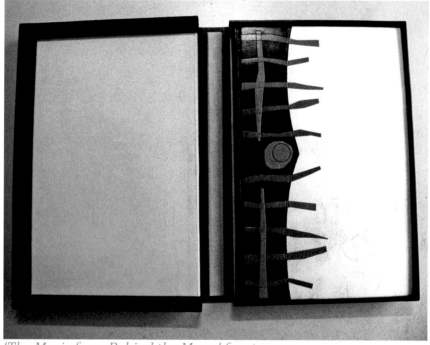

'The Music from Behind the Moon' front cover.

'The Music From Behind the Moon'

hearth fire, it is drowned by the piping voices of our children. We being human, may pause to listen now and then, half wistfully, it may be for an unrememberable cadence which only the young hear."

My binding is in vellum and black goatskin with my design impression within. Tooled in blind small circles, with onlays in mid grey reaching out and orange onlays suggesting behind the moon. The leaves are sewn together on five Irish linen tapes with an attractive mid grey endpaper. It is housed in an up and over protective box, covered in black buckram and lined inside with suede. The title is hand lettered in real gold along the spine.

From Paradise to Lucker Street.
The Story Before Wongawill. By Patsy and Ian Patterson.

The story behind a family's emigration from a Northumbrian village to distant Australia. The story of three streets and the people who lived there; whether they emigrated to the coal mines, coke furnaces or steel works of New South Wales, moving to Yorkshire and beyond, they are still my people, your people, our people: This is our story.

'From Paradise to Lucker Street' full panel.

'From Paradise to Lucker Street' is a most difficult binding to date, I hope it works for Patsy and Ian Patterson. I really have tried my level best; it is a personal story and a personal binding. I am satisfied by the outcome. The feeling of my binding is all atmosphere, starting from the inside end leaves, edge decoration using acrylic paints to harmonize with the choice of leather goatskin covering, cover design, blind tooling, suede flyleaves and endpapers.

For 'From Paradise to Lucker Street' I have included two Lacunose panels. A most original binding, everything tones in and matches tastefully. I have made a protective up and over box, covered with a sympathetic matching art buckram, claret wine colour and lined in oxford blue suede. Titled in '36 point' handled letters along the box spine and front, matching with the spine of the goatskin binding. A full title in real gold on the front of the box.

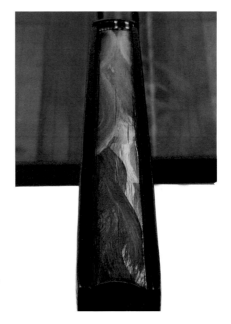

Promised for Easter, I have kept my promise. A most important Delrue special binding of 200 man hours, for the authors Patsy and Ian.

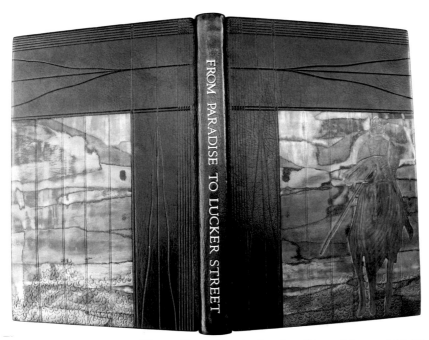

'From Paradise to Lucker Street' bound 2009.

Le Grand Meaulnes. *By Henri Alain-Fournier.*

Translated by Frank Davison, illustrated by Laura Carlin. The Folio Society 2008. Printed on Abbey wove paper at T.J. International, Cornwall.

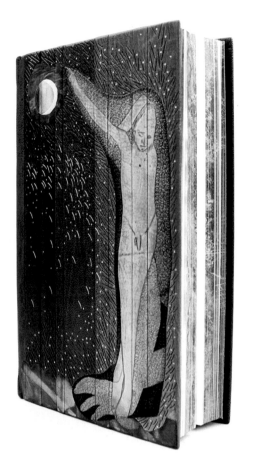

'Le Grand Meaulnes' was first published in 1913 by Emile-Paul Freres in Paris. The most illuminating factor of Henri Alain-Fournier's novel 'Le Grand Meaulnes' is its unequalled atmosphere of mystery and romance, which was footed in actuality. The imaginary landscape evoked so fastidiously, is the simple background to his life at home, in the valley of the Cher.

Henri Alain-Fournier was born in 1886 at Chapelle d'Angillon with its flatness, its monotonous horizon, where the level of the land hid three quarters sky, a little like the Cambridge Fens, or the fields of Norfolk. This curious countryside formed the background of his novel for he was killed in the First World War.

Meaulnes is a simple story about schoolboys in the French countryside, whose main activity is to run away from school, get lost and fall rather helplessly in love. Try to see it through the eyes of childhood, with its blend of love, dream and adventure; it captures the haunted atmosphere of this remote and isolated

corner of ancient France. The school background, the wintery atmosphere, its abandoned marshes and decaying chateaux. He wrote it at the height of perfection and purity, which I shall never again attain.

> *'That is the Land of Lost Content,*
> *I see it shining plain,*
> *The happy highways where I went*
> *And cannot come again.'*

My Binding is in full 'Harmatan' goatskin using my Tudor style in colours of mid green, light brown, tan, grey, silver and black, with the figure of Augustino Meaulnes. I depicted seasonal colours with black tooling and a gold leaf windshape decoration.

232

'Le Grand Meaulnes'

Augustin always seemed to travel at night time, by the light of the moon. Inside the board his travels continue with my binding. It has several colour endleaves and suede flyleaves of sunny green.

The book edges are coloured using acrylics in seasonal colours, browns, greens, whites, pale reds and oranges. It is housed in an up and over box which I have covered in warm grey, with a pale green suede inside for added protection. The box and front cover have been titled in black hand letters, (936 point).

It was bound in springtime at my bindery, Crispin, Ruthin, North Wales in 2010.

The Boy in the Striped Pyjamas.
A fable by John Boyne.

'The Boy in the Striped Pyjamas'

This edition was published 2006 by David Fickling Books, of Random House Children's Books and is signed by the author. John Boyne was born in Ireland in 1971 and studied at Trinity College, Dublin.

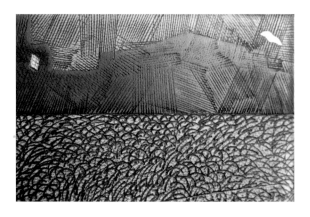

'The Boy in the Striped Pyjamas' is a very difficult story to describe. If you do start to read this book, you will find yourself on a journey with a nine year old boy called Bruno;

235

Front cover.

Endleaves.

though this isn't a book for nine year olds. And sooner or later you will arrive with Bruno at a fence; fences like this exist all over the world. I hope you never have to encounter such a fence.

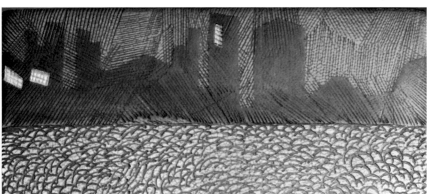

Back cover landscape (above) and edge colour detail (below).

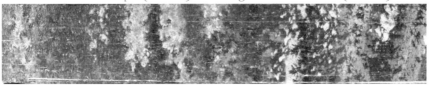

Top edge colouring.

Lacunose face in detail.

Bound in a dull and worn grey goatskin, overcast into sections then sewn on four Irish linen tapes. The book edges are again coloured using acrylics with shades of grey, dark red, yellow (for the windows), white and black.

Mottled grey suede doublures.

238

'Tree of Life'

Silver grey headbands, onlays of dark blue, lit windows and a figure of a boy at a fence in striped pyjamas. The book is housed in a protective box.

I have been overwhelmed and moved when designing this book. The design was my most difficult in all of my long years binding books. I hope those that feel and touch the book are just as moved.

239

'The Boy in the Striped Pyjamas'

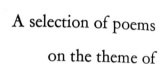

A selection of poems

on the theme of

WATER

240

The design for 'Water' was inspired by an old photograph of me leaving the sea on Clacton beach. It was taken by my holiday friend Ian Macgregor in the hot summer of 1960 on my box brownie camera. We had just been to the end of the pier to see the British crooner Michael Holliday singing his hits; 'Story of my Life' and 'Starry Eyed'. Ian and I both needed to be refreshed after the performance and so we took a dip in the water on a warm evening in July.

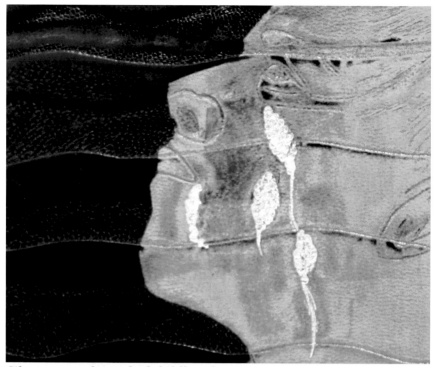

243   *Silver tears; the end of childhood.*

244

Paul coming out of the water, Clacton 1960.

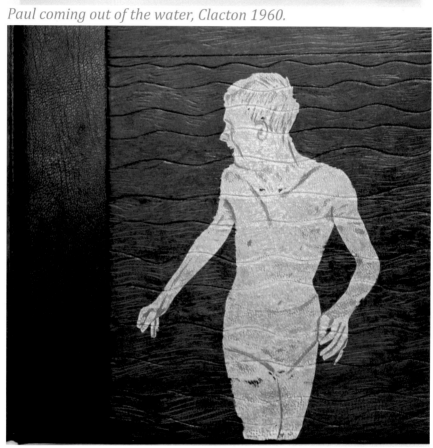

Paul's face (close up) and top edge colouring.

246

Moonlight over Miami.

247

New Bookbinding Techniques.
An Artistic Invention: My Lacunose and Tudor styles.

I completed my first lacunose binding in my Chester workshop in 1985. The binding was the biography of Blair Hughes-Stanton. I had over many years been experimenting with leather in the form of leather pictures. My work up to this point had been mostly illustrative, whereby I used many leather onlays to express myself. I had always thought of this approach as somewhat similar to 'painting by numbers' which can often appear rather childish. For a long time I had wondered how I could achieve a more naturalistic effect when working in leather.

The work continues: My current Ruthin Bindery.

One weekend, I had forwarded the Hughes-Stanton book up to the covering stage. I then decided, in a flash, to do something I had long wanted to do, which was to apply a piece of leather directly on top of the millboard. I used paste and PVA to apply the leather. I overlapped some more pieces of leather and I puckered others, in a random fashion. When I'd finished, and achieved the overall effect I wanted on both front and back

My new haven.

covers, difficulties emerged, in that my montage whilst pleasing to the eye, was structurally impractical. I felt so uncomfortable with what I'd done that I decided to sleep on it.

Fortunately the next day was Sunday, a quiet day as usual. Looking at the book anew, I thought the best way for the boards to open and close would be to give the whole thing a sand papering, something I had never dared to do on a binding until this point. I started off with a rough sandpaper and ended with a smooth one. The sand papering on the Hughes-Stanton occupied me all day. When the leather began to lift a little, it became obvious to apply, at intervals a very watery PVA. I quickly appreciated that no sanding could be done until the watery PVA had dried.

Near the end of the day's laborious sanding and PVAing, I noticed the most wonderful effects that the various leathers had, and to my surprise the book began to function beautifully: The opening and closing, the headcap and the turn-ins proved most satisfactory. The next day, I added some blind decoration directly onto the cover and in four weeks time it was snapped up by Prof. John Burton of Bristol.

It was my first ever lacunose binding, since then I have completed over thirty using this technique. Up to this point, the technique has been known as 'Sanding and PVAing'. It was only when I bound another book ten years later that a friend from Liverpool University decided that we really must put this technique together, and he called it 'lacunose' meaning 'furrowed' or 'pitted'.

The technique.

The following is a summary of the procedures (and pitfalls) of this marvellous technique which I hope will encourage others to try it:

Choose your leather.

I find that Harmatan leather works better than any other for lacunose. Harmatan's skins have rare and brilliant colours hidden away inside them, colours which are only revealed through sanding. Every piece of leather reveals different colours when sanded.

'Kyffin, A Celebration'

Preparation.

Best results can be achieved for the beginner by practising on a piece of board rather than a binding. Brockman some pieces of leather, whatever scraps you can find. Apply the leather directly onto the board (including turn-ins) with a 50/50 PVA-paste mix.

As you apply the pieces, vary the pattern of application, overlapping some pieces, puckering others, putting some directly on top of others. Interestingly, the hornier the leather, the more interesting the results. After covering, wait at least an hour to dry in the press or under a light weight.

253

Sanding.

Begin sanding tentatively with a rough grit paper. When the leather begins to become thin it will start to lift away from the board. At this point apply a coating of watery PVA, about 1/4 tsp in 1/2 cup of water and let it dry for 1 hour.

Sand again with next finest grit. Apply watery PVA again, let dry, then sand.

The number of times you repeat the process will vary depending on the look you are going for and how pleased you are with the patterns emerging. If you are unhappy with the design,

you can apply new leather pieces, and continue (this is especially helpful if you want to hide completely a shape or colour that does not work).

Pressing.
Pressing between sandings is not always necessary, but can achieve the effect of compacting the leather layers already applied, making way for possible applications of new pieces.
After you've done the panel and are happy, put the completed lacunose panel in between Formica boards overnight, under light pressure. This imparts a wonderful sheen to the leather. When pressed, the surface will be very smooth to the touch, with interesting pits and furrows below the surface.

Headcaps and turn-ins.
Before the lacunose process begins, the headcaps are covered in the usual way, as if for a full binding. Leather pieces are then applied up to but not over the caps.
Leather pieces can be applied over the turn-ins and corners

during the lacunose procedure.
The board edges and turn-ins are then sanded and PVAed along with the boards.

Variations.
After the final pressing, any blind or gold tooling can be carried out. The lacunosed leather can be as dark as you want, or, with extra sanding (and less PVAing) you can lighten the tones.
If you want a lacunosed panel as part of a conventionally covered binding, or as part of a larger design, apply thin layers of leather to a piece of archival aid paper, off the book, and then drop it in as a panel.

If carried out with care and patience, lacunose gives a result that is successful and pleasing, and gives the book an atmosphere that no other design approach can achieve.

255

'Firearms' bound in 1988.

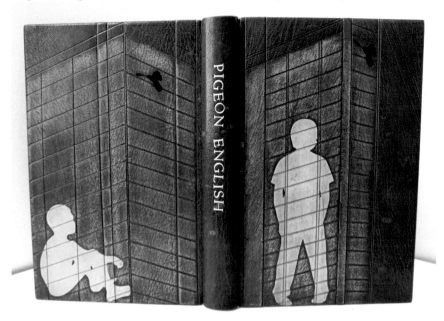

Tudor Style.

A new artistic style of binding which acquired its name from the first book I bound in this way; Shakespeare's Sonnets. Put simply, it is made by covering the boards with a series of overlapping strips of goatskin, which create built-up areas on the boards similar to those achieved by the traditional built-up board technique, but without the need to build up the board underneath, and without the need for scarf joints where two pieces of leather meet.

The technique.

Preparation.

The book is covered as for a quarter binding, i.e. the spine and part of the boards are covered with goatskin.

The leather on the boards is thinned, but still maintains its strength (not as thin as a label, for instance, but thinner than would be used for covering in full leather).

The edge of the leather is then cut in a clean edge, without a bevel, either straight down the book or at an angle that you want for your design.

'A Season in Hell'

Application.

Paste out and apply the first leather strip to the book.

Another strip of leather is pared, and then the edge that is to overlap is edge-pared at a sharp bevel (45°).

This is then pasted out and laid over the first strip, and where the two strips overlap a new raised strip will be formed.

The other edge is cut without a bevel, to create the next edge to be overlapped, and so on.

Finishing.

The overlapping pieces can be as large or small as you want. The feel of the leather, particularly where it overlaps, is very attractive. The lines where the strips overlap can be tooled or emphasized with the use of a sharp bone folder.

The finished binding has the look of having been wrapped in leather, bandage-style. But rather than calling it 'overlapping bandage style,' I thought it would be a good idea to give it a proper name, and 'Tudor Style' seemed to fit.

Paul's Favourite Bindings.

Here is a very small selection of my favourite bindings and leather pictures from over the years:

'Jude the Obscure'

260

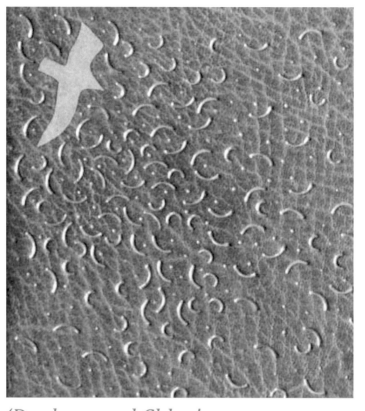

261

'Daphnes and Chloe'

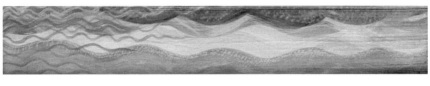

'A Shrophire Lad' by A.E. Housman, bound in Ruthin 2009.

263

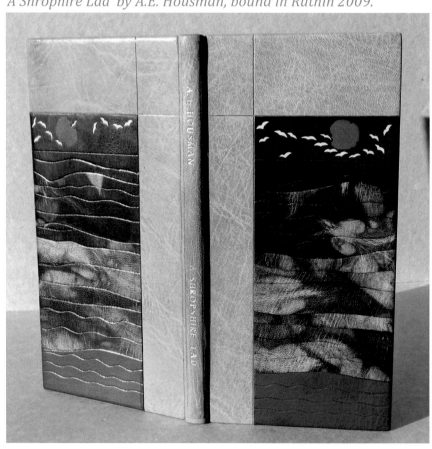

'Silver Tears of Life'

Eating a crispy bacon sandwich before school, St Joseph's 1958.

JOHN CLARE
VERSES FOR
HIS CHILDREN

266

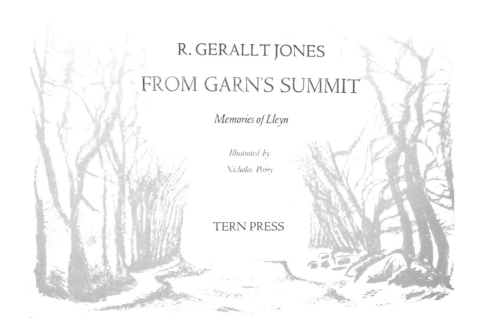

R. GERALLT JONES

FROM GARN'S SUMMIT

Memories of Lleyn

Illustrated by
Nicholas Parry

TERN PRESS

LIKE A RIVER

Within me
    & around

your being is like a river
        that flows
                unheard

in a valley
        that's green

because you're at its centre

268

269

'Mapping Golgotha' by Wilfred Owen, bound in Ruthin 2010.

270

'Y Deuddeg' (Paul's confessional) bound in Ruthin 2010.

'Mosaic' leather picture (above) and 'Alice in Wonderland'.

272

'Peter Pan'

273

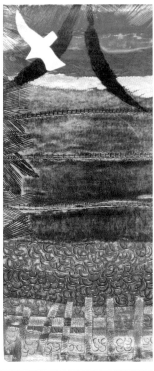

TWENTY POEMS OF WALKING

275

'Daydreaming'

'Comus' bound in 1994.

In 1989 I celebrated the fall of the Berlin Wall by binding 'Perestroika'. At last Germany was united and I was exited for the first time that the politicians had done the right thing. If only the whole world was at peace and not fighting and killing whoever gets in their way. Our leaders in the world of now, seem to fight selfishly for their cause using the words 'God is on my side'.

Roll the Credits.

This is the final chapter of my book 'My Soul Has No Friends' and as I look back over these few leaves, I still feel unrewarded. Most of the people I write about have been 'gathered in' and still I don't have the answers I seek. What makes me the way I am, why do I think the way I do and more importantly what makes me tick? I have felt a strong need to write my book and to look over my shoulder, remembering the faces of those I love, re-visiting people and places that captured my imagination. My memory is clear, especially that of my childhood; that strong emotion that I truly loved and have carried with me throughout my life. There is never a day when my feelings do not return to the secure and happy times of those Feltham and Enfield boys' homes. I return, asking myself simple questions again and again. What are reasons for wanting to know answers? I keep asking why me, and what makes me the person I am? I have not made an impact, but do any of us? In the mornings I wake up happy to be alive, returning to my warm, comfortable Bindery, still to be working, binding family treasures, 'thinking', listening to my beloved Delius and remembering my past.

I met Les Parsons, a helper in the home, when I lived at St Joseph's Boys' Home in Enfield. He was kind and helpful, but I also felt him to be a man of wise words, all the kids liked him and he made a big difference to our early lives. Years later I arranged to meet him for a drink in London, Victoria, near where he worked, to talk and remember the past. The pub was called 'The Green Man', a large Victorian pub with bright coloured glass doors. We greeted each other with a warm shaking of hands, and a hug.

"Well Paul, how very nice to see you again, are you still binding books for University College?" he asked.

"Yes and I love it, in fact it is the perfect job." I answered.

"I remember you as I do Jimmy McMahon. You and Jimmy made and decorated a large rug with Hugh Maynard (another of the helpers). You also painted very well with water colours and made many beautiful baskets for the old ladies, who were very happy to pay half a crown towards the craft materials. Ron Arbetta was a great influence on you, more than any of the other boys. He often talked about you and the hand talents you had. He said you always came to crafts naturally. I remember you made, with difficulty, a beautiful pair of gloves which won a national competition. Ron was very proud. But you Paul, I singled you out as one of the boys who would do well in life once you left the boys' home in Enfield."

"But Les, how would you know that? I was like all the other kids, I never knew the difference."

"It was late Sunday evening, you would have been about thirteen years old, slight and fair, I looked at the way you kicked the rubber ball around in the playground, you moved it around beautifully, it was that I liked, you danced football. As soon as you saw me watching you, you suddenly stopped to pull your socks up, looking up at me, giving me a big wide smile. I remember being quite touched. I handed you the weekly St Joseph's Newsletter, you politely thanked me, putting the newsletter, rolled up, into your trouser pocket. You then ran off towards the other kids, who were still kicking the worn old rubber tennis ball around. It was then I clearly marked you out Paul, you see it was the way that you pulled your grey socks up. You seemed always to make the best of everything, I bet you still do? Have another drink on me Paul, whatever you want."

"Thanks Les, I will have Teachers double Scotch please."

"I think I will join you." he said.

We left The Green Man pub with a magic glow. Talking to Les made me feel excited and renewed. I loved that evening and kept Les's words in my heart. It was the last time I saw him. I think of you often in my dreams Les. I'm writing my book, it's mostly about childhood and growing up. I keep returning to the reason for writing it. It is a journey through my life, seeking answers about what makes me tick and who I am. Most of the people I write about have died, and you Les were gathered in three years ago, it made me weep remembering their faces, those who have pulled me through. What I am is perhaps what they made me.

I cannot face rejection again, that's why I cannot visit my brother and sister. They live with their families in Coventry. They are from my father's side of the family. I have their address but I am simply afraid to knock on their doors in case they shut me out, I'm not sure I can face that. A brother and sister I have never met. Perhaps they have the answers that I have been seeking for so long. I wonder what they look like? Shall I ever know? My father Jack Spencer Payne rejected me, his son. I would have loved a father.

"I just need to end my book, I have to come to the end of my journey it is as simple as that Les."

What about the hurt? The kids who did not make it, who were pushed into loneliness and misery? Who will end their lives? Such pain I have never known. Perhaps you Les gave me the only answer. When you said simply;

"Paul, it was the way you pulled your socks up, you were different from the start, you made the best of things."

Les, I remember I looked up at you and smiled, it is that simple. So ends my few leaves, my book, still looking for answers, why me?

Paulie, pull your socks up, smile and be happy.

282

fin

...of the past: Gus Conte, Seamus
...nces Howlett, David Hea...
...on Colston, Micheal O'B...
...Quinn, John Potter, Ange...
...Eddie Satherthwaite, ...
...O'Connor, Michael Doch...
...rie Damon, Jimmy Ashto...
...Michael Lynch, Jeremy Pau...
...aldron, Peter Jones, Geor...
...ohn Delaney, Lawrence Ga...
...ields, Ian Crangle, Miss Ma...
...vinSeaward, Harry Mills, B...
...tephen Lamb, Terry Kara...
...Ryan, Philip Donneky, Jo...
...rawly, Mr Mash, Kevin
...d Shaw, Sister Louise, J...
...Holmes, Chris Steven...
...Nicky Crangle, M...
...Escarcelle, Brian H...
...ony Kavanah, A. Papazoglo...

, Margaret Magill, Ted Watkins, Hugh Parsons, Sister Barnard, Paul Herlihy, ed Lanragin, Christopher Sims, Richard to, Robert Kingwood, Christopher Shaw, Iolden, John Grange, Philip Coyle, Antho- n Chambers, Patrick Callahan, Michael r Winter, Bishop Craven, Philip Langley, orge Atkinson, Christopher Melia, Penny b, Pat Reid, Michael Harrington, Jimmy Ian Macgregor, David Jacobs, David Ca- Michael O'Halleran, Michael Saunders, d Richie, Robin Dines, Tommy Terry, Ter- , Peter Franklin, Peter Donneky, Charlie Pearson, Stella Shaw, Tony Ramm, Tony rty, John Minihane, David Rutter, Jason enn, Tony Hawes, Stephen Timlin, Paul- ss Annie, Susan Filipi, John Grace, Miss ary, Paul Pentony, Richard Grace, Little , Terence Baldock, Tommy Driscoll, Miss Alexander, Miss Louie and Budgie Joey.

Boys' Club Members w Handicraft Prizes 1958

"I never heard a child enjoying itself. There was nearly always someone crying, somebody getting a beating for nothing"